The Twilight Zone Scripts of Jerry Sohl

The Twilight Zone Scripts of Jerry Sohl

Edited by Christopher Conlon

BearManor Media
2004

The Twilight Zone Scripts of Jerry Sohl
Copyright © 2004 by the Estate of Jerry Sohl.
All rights reserved.

"Introduction: Jerry Sohl and *The Twilight Zone*" copyright © 2004
by Christopher Conlon.

"Afterword: A Touch of Strange" copyright © 2004
by George Clayton Johnson.

Published in the USA by
Bear Manor Media
P. O. Box 71426
Albany, GA 31708

bearmanormedia.com

Editor's website: christopherconlon.com

Cover design by John Teehan
Typesetting and layout by John Teehan

Library of Congress Cataloging-in-Publication Data

Sohl, Jerry.
The Twilight Zone scripts of Jerry Sohl / by the Estate of Jerry Sohl.
p. cm.
"'Introduction: Jerry Sohl and The Twilight Zone' by Christopher Conlon; 'Afterword: A Touch of Strange' by George Clayton Johnson."
ISBN 1-59393-010-0

1. Fantasy drama, American. 2. Television plays, American. I. Twilight zone (Television program) II. Title.

PS3569.O4T88 2004
812'.54--dc22
2004017061

ISBN 1-59393-010-0

Library of Congress Control No. 2004103576

For Tony Albarella

Table of Contents

Introduction: Jerry Sohl and *The Twilight Zone* 1
   by Christopher Conlon

The New Exhibit 7

Living Doll 87

Queen of the Nile 131

Afterword: A Touch of Strange 173
   by George Clayton Johnson

Acknowledgments 177

Introduction: Jerry Sohl and *The Twilight Zone*
by Christopher Conlon

When Jerry Sohl passed away in November of 2002, newspaper obituaries across the country listed as his primary credits his novels of the 1950s (*Point Ultimate, The Altered Ego*) along with scripts for *Star Trek, Alfred Hitchcock Presents*—and *The Twilight Zone*. That the last title was included at all is a testament to the unusual legacy which Sohl left to the program. One of his *Twilight Zone* works, "Living Doll" (in which Erich Streator is terrorized by his stepdaughter's "Talky Tina"), is a perennial fan favorite which invariably scores near the top in any poll of the program's all-time best episodes. And yet, until the early 1980s, few had any idea that Sohl had even contributed to the series—for the simple reason that his name never appeared in the credits.

Watch "Living Doll" today—or "The New Exhibit," or "Queen of the Nile"—and you will see that the byline reads, "Written by Charles Beaumont."

Beaumont, of course, was the brilliant fantasist who penned dozens of classic short stories, scripts for films such as *The Seven Faces of Dr. Lao* and *The Wonderful World of the Brothers Grimm*—and numerous episodes of *The Twilight Zone*. Suffering the effects of an early onslaught of Alzheimer's disease, Beaumont by 1963 was still able to talk his way into television assignments, but was no longer able to complete the scripts. As a result, his friends—including Jerry Sohl—stepped in, working as ghost writers to help keep the Beaumont family together and the medical bills paid. It was in every way a noble gesture on the part of these men (other Beaumont ghosts included George Clayton Johnson, John Tomerlin and OCee

Ritch), but, ironically, it would rob Jerry Sohl of public acknowledgment for some of his greatest achievements.

Though audiences were unaware of the subterranean goings-on at the time, Sohl's family was entirely cognizant of the situation. "Everyone knew there was something wrong with Chuck," Jean Sohl, Jerry's widow, says today. She was perfectly aware that her husband had agreed to be a ghost-writer for the ailing Beaumont. "I was Jerry's editor, after all," she says. "I corrected his grammar and spelling and made any suggestions I thought of. I remember that I especially liked 'Living Doll.'" The Sohls' children knew, as well. Their daughter Jennifer has a childhood memory of being with some friends who were discussing an episode of *The Twilight Zone* when she said, "My dad really wrote that." But at the time neither she nor her friends thought it was particularly important.

The ghosting was a simple process. Sohl and Beaumont would generally meet in a local restaurant, where they tossed around possible story ideas. Once a basic concept had been agreed upon, they would flesh out the major plot points. Then it was Beaumont's job to pitch the idea to *Twilight Zone*'s producers. After it was accepted, Sohl would write the script, splitting the money evenly with Beaumont.

A good example of the process is "The New Exhibit," Sohl's first script for the series, an hour-long excursion into horror produced in the program's fourth season.

"One of the men in the script is the man that gave Chuck the idea for the script itself, Albert W. Hicks, the ax murderer," Jerry Sohl said in an interview for *The Twilight Zone Companion*. "So we got to talking about, 'Well, supposing that someone had an exhibit wherein this murderer was, and he came alive and did all this and then went back to the exhibit after he committed the murder. The police would never be able to find him.' This was the way our minds went. Then we decided to change that and make it that they were *all* murderers, this is the murderers' exhibit."

Though the manuscript of the version published here is marked "First Rough Draft," it will quickly become clear to any fan of the episode that it was filmed almost exactly as written. The finished program adds some dialogue to two scenes (probably written by Beaumont, who generally completed any requested revisions on the scripts), and the early sections of the final act are rearranged slightly. Overall, however, Sohl could only have been delighted with the finished product, even if it did not bear his name.

"The New Exhibit" has suffered over the years, however, due to a persistent confusion about what happens at the climax. Perhaps because the finished episode bears a certain generic resemblance to *Psycho*—it even stars Martin Balsam, who played the private investigator, Arbogast, in Hitchcock's film—there has been an assumption on the part of some critics as to the identity of the "real" murderer in this story. But this is a misunderstanding that close readers of the script should have no problem correcting—just as they should be able to see exactly why this underrated gem was such a perfect script for *The Twilight Zone*.

Sohl went on to contribute two more works which the series produced in its fifth and final season (by which time it had reverted to its original half-hour format). The status of "Living Doll" as a timeless classic has been attested to by any number of writers over the years ("One of the high points of television history," asserts Marc Zicree, author of *The Twilight Zone Companion*), not to mention by its endless, inevitably inferior imitators. "Living Doll" was not the first killer-doll tale ever written (Algernon Blackwood was there many years earlier), but, like several installments of the series, it represents the ultimate treatment of a particular theme. Murderous dolls come and go, but the line "My name is Talky Tina, and I'm going to kill you" lives on in the dreams and nightmares of practically anyone who has ever seen the episode.

Interestingly, as the script in this volume reveals, the original conception of Talky Tina was quite different from that of the completed program. Specifically described in Sohl's script as an "ugly" doll fully half the little girl's size, the intention seems to have been to make Talky Tina repellent and even monstrous from her very first appearance on screen. In production, however, a different approach prevailed—to create a small, beautiful doll, highlighting the awful contrast between her sweet appearance and the terrible things she says. The final episode also adds considerably to the dialogue between Erich Streator and Talky Tina, making the doll a more developed character than Sohl's shadowy, menacing being. Reading the script, it is fascinating to imagine how the segment might have played without the revisions—possibly it would have been darker and even more intense. But there is no question that the final episode is a masterpiece, and that Jerry Sohl's script was the key to the success of the entire enterprise.

"Queen of the Nile," his final piece produced for *The Twilight Zone*, is often criticized as a rehash of Beaumont's own earlier episode, "Long Live Walter Jameson." But this well-crafted tale has resonances that are Sohl's own. Unlike "The New Exhibit" or "Living Doll," the idea for the story was completely Sohl's, based on a scarab ring he once owned. "Someone found that scarab ring and gave it to me," Sohl told interviewer Matthew R. Bradley. " 'Here's something for you,' " the giver told him. " 'It's really scary.' " Sohl recognized the scarab as the Egyptian symbol of immortality, and decided, "What the hell, this is an interesting ring. Let's write a story about it."

In fact, Sohl wrote two stories. The first, "Trefelgen's Ring," was finished in the late 1950s, but did not see the light of print until the retrospective volume *Filet of Sohl: The Classic Scripts and Stories of Jerry Sohl* (Bear Manor Media, 2003). In 1963 he produced a very different take on the idea with "Queen of the Nile." "They shot it exactly the way I wrote it," Sohl said later. "That one, also, was a lot of fun to do, and I think they did a good job on it."

Sohl wrote two more scripts for *The Twilight Zone,* but at this point the series was winding down and these efforts, "Pattern for Doomsday" and "Who Am I?," were not produced. This pair of "almost *Zone*s" would not see the light of day until 2003, with the publication of the *Filet of Sohl* volume.

In the years since Marc Zicree revealed Sohl's role in the program in *The Twilight Zone Companion*, some efforts have been made to give the author the recognition he deserves. In the liner notes for various video releases of the series, Sohl's name is properly credited. Sohl himself gave numerous interviews in the last twenty years of his life in which he discussed the program and his role in it. And now, with the publication of this collection, Jerry Sohl's name can finally be added to the distinguished *Twilight Zone* bookshelf, proudly alongside Rod Serling, Richard Matheson, George Clayton Johnson, Earl Hamner, and Charles Beaumont.

"Good writing," Sohl once said, "is in the eye and the mind of the writer and reader." These scripts, all examples of very good writing, will live in the eye and the mind of everyone who reads them. Now, at last, we can celebrate the wonderful mind that truly wrote them.

THE TWILIGHT ZONE

The New Exhibit

Living Doll

Queen of the Nile

Written by Jerry Sohl for Charles Beaumont in an agreement centered on his increasing difficulties in writing because of Alzheimer's disease which he did not then know he had; the work was done to aid Chuck and his family.

> – Jerry Sohl,
> *undated note located in the author's*
> Twilight Zone *files*

The New Exhibit

Original Airdate: April 4, 1963

THE NEW EXHIBIT

FADE IN:

EXT. MUSEUM—LONG SHOT—DAY

An old mansion that must have been in its day a showplace, set back from the street, its ornateness incongruous in a more functional world. CAMERA PANS to a sign on the lawn: FERGUSON'S MUSEUM.

INT. MUSEUM—CLOSE SHOT—JACK THE RIPPER

The wax effigy of Jack the Ripper is startlingly lifelike in this gloomy chamber, illuminated by an overhead spotlight. The Ripper's left hand is to one side, ready to make a sweeping motion to cut a throat with the knife it holds; his eyes are alight with mad hilarity. CAMERA DRAWS BACK to show the figure, medium height, square-built, dark-complexioned, clean-shaven, in a long black overcoat and soft felt hat. CAMERA WHIP PANS to a door where MR. FERGUSON appears, half a dozen PATRONS behind him. He turns to them.

REVERSE ANGLE—GROUP SHOT

Ferguson, a large, balding, ordinarily cheerful man in his 60s, faces the patrons gravely. Over his head is a sign: MURDERER'S ROW.

> FERGUSON
> ...and now our next group—our *piece de resistance*, if I may say so—here you will find

the most infamous, black-hearted killers of all
time. It is not for the faint-hearted, so...
            (elaborate chuckle)
if there are any who would prefer to stay behind
...No?

There are a few polite titters and some of the patrons look at each other in amusement.

                    FERGUSON
                (turning to go in)
            Very well, then...

ANGLE TO DOOR

The patrons enter with Ferguson, their steps echoing hollowly. CAMERA MOVES WITH THEM and DRAWS AHEAD TO QUICKLY PAN the exhibit: Jack the Ripper; Henri Desire Landru, a middle-aged man with a thin nose, high bald head, flowing drab beard and deep-sunken eyes, holding a waxed cord out before him, ready to garrote, his eyes flaming with evil; Burke and Hare, with Burke smothering a figure on a bed with a pillow, Hare holding the victim's feet, Burke being undersized, thick-set, round, with an unlined faced, inadequate nose, Hare, tall and thin, face pointed, eyes wide-set and slanting; and Albert Hicks, a burly man of 40 in a seaman's outfit, standing with an upraised gleaming ax about to sink it into the skull of MARTIN SENESCU, a man of about 50 with wisps of graying hair and gentle eyes.

ANGLE PAST GROUP IN F.G.

as they assemble and TOWARD Hicks and Martin as Martin, seeming to be a part of the exhibit, makes an imperceptible, minute adjustment to Hicks' costume.

                    FERGUSON
            This is Martin Senescu, curator of Murderer's
            Row.

Martin suddenly moves. A YOUNG GIRL draws back with a gasp, a YOUNG MAN'S arm going protectively around her. Martin stands, steps down toward the velvet rope that protects the figures from the spectators. He smiles.

> MARTIN
> (not at all sorry)
> Did I startle you?

GROUP—FAVORING YOUNG COUPLE

The young man looks at her worriedly.

> YOUNG MAN
> You all right, honey?

> GIRL
> (slightly embarrassed)
> Sure, it's just…they're so real—and I thought—

> YOUNG MAN
> Aah, they're just a lotta wax. Nothing to be afraid of.

SHOT—MARTIN

Irked by the remark.

> MARTIN
> (professionally sinister)
> Perhaps not, young man. But who can tell what evil lurks in the heart of the man standing next to you?

CAMERA DRAWS BACK to INCLUDE Hicks. Martin turns to him.

                    MARTIN
　　Albert W. Hicks, mate of the oyster-smack E.A.
　　Johnson—a gentle man. Yet one day in 1860
　　off the Atlantic Coast, he murdered everyone in
　　his crew, killed them with an ax exactly like this
　　one. Why did he go mad? What made him change?

CAMERA MOVES with Martin to Burke and Hare.

                    MARTIN
                (almost affectionate)
　　Burke and Hare, the monsters of their time. But
　　do they look like monsters? Oh, if we knew them
　　perhaps we'd understand the torment that drove
　　these worthies from shoemaking into the work
　　of ghouls so late in their lives. You see here how
　　they suffocated their victims—it was called burking.
　　Think of the agonies they and their victims must
　　have endured!

CAMERA MOVES with Martin to Landru, whom he regards benignly.

                    MARTIN
　　Henri Desire Landru!…So filled with love and
　　hate…He loved nearly three hundred women in
　　his lifetime…his letters are filled with tenderness
　　and feeling…

PAN SHOT—PATRONS' FACES

Nervousness, boredom, disdain, fear, fascination.

                    MARTIN
　　…One can see the agony that he, too, must
　　have felt as he was driven to strangle the life
　　from disappointed spinsters and lonely widows
　　…Landru was a master of the garrote and he
　　used a wax cord identical to the one he holds here.

BACK TO MARTIN

                  MARTIN
It was his executioner who gave Landru the peace he sought in life.

CAMERA MOVES with Martin to Jack the Ripper.

                  MARTIN
Another soul in torment, Jack the Ripper. Who was he? Which among all the faces that moved about London's Whitechapel district was his? And why did he feel driven to kill those pathetic drabs with one sweep of the knife you see here across their throats?

ANOTHER ANGLE

as Martin moves closer to Jack the Ripper and stands in the path of the knife.

                  MARTIN
I am afraid we shall never know. As we look at Hicks, Burke and Hare, at Landru and Jack the Ripper, we see men like you and me, and we can only guess what devils pushed them to their bloody fate...
                  (beat)
Thank you.

Martin bows.

                                            CUT TO:

CLOSE SHOT—MARTIN'S FOOT

It moves to and presses a button on the dias floor.

CUT TO:

MED. SHOT—MARTIN

As he reaches the low point of his bow, Jack the Ripper's arm whips out in a wide sweep in a swishing motion with the knife, then jerks back into place as the patrons gasp and Martin straightens to smile at them.

SHOT—SERLING

> SERLING
> Martin Senescu, a gentle man, the dedicated curator of Murderers' Row in Ferguson's Wax Museum. He ponders the reasons why ordinary men are driven to commit mass murder. What Mr. Senescu does not know is that the groundwork has already been laid for his own special kind of madness, and torment found only in The Twilight Zone.

FADE OUT

FADE IN:

INT. MUSEUM—MURDERER'S ROW—MED. SHOT—MARTIN

Humming to himself, Martin uses a clothes brush on Landru's suit, picking off a piece of lint we can't see, regarding Landru critically, albeit lovingly.

ANGLE TO DOORWAY

Ferguson appears there, stops to watch Martin O.S. His face betrays that he has something unpleasant to discuss. He starts off toward Martin.

ANGLE PAST MARTIN IN F.G.

and TOWARD the approaching Ferguson. Martin has turned up the collar of Landru's coat, whisks it gently, unaware of Ferguson's presence. Ferguson stops, regards Martin before he speaks. Then:

> FERGUSON
> Martin.

MARTIN

Pauses in his work to look at Ferguson O.S., the brush poised.

> MARTIN
> Yes, Mr. Ferguson?

FERGUSON

There is no other way; he must get it out. Not unkindly:

> FERGUSON
> I'd like to talk to you.

> MARTIN'S VOICE
> I'll be through here in a moment.

> FERGUSON
> It can wait. What I have to say is…rather important.

MARTIN AND FERGUSON

Martin stops his work, a little annoyed at the interruption but sensing something more than routine.

> MARTIN
> Oh?

He looks back to Landru, adjusts the collar, takes a couple swipes at the sleeves, eyes the figure critically for a moment.

                    MARTIN
            You know, I think Landru needs a new suit.
            This one is ten years old and shows it.

When Ferguson does not answer, Martin looks toward him, steps down, puts aside his brush and cloth, turns to him.

                    MARTIN
            Is something wrong?

                    FERGUSON
            Well, yes—and no…I think we'd better discuss
            it in the office.

Ferguson starts off. Martin looks after him worriedly, then, after a final, cursory look at Landru, moves after Ferguson, frowning.

INT. FERGUSON'S OFFICE—ANGLE TO DOOR

An old office filled with small figures, spotlighted busts, photographs of current and previous exhibits. The door opens, Ferguson comes in, followed by Martin. CAMERA FOLLOWS them to the desk as Martin says:

                    MARTIN
            Is it something I've done—or haven't done?

Ferguson takes his chair, Martin standing uneasily to one side.

                    FERGUSON
            No, no. Nothing like that.
                    (beat)
            Sit down.

Martin sinks slowly to a chair, staring at Ferguson blankly. Ferguson eyes him solemnly. After a pause:

                    FERGUSON
            Martin, I'm abandoning the museum.

CLOSE SHOT—MARTIN

He can't believe his ears. Of all the words in the world, these are the ones he hoped he'd never hear. He shakes his head dazedly.

>   MARTIN
> Abandoning—
>
>   FERGUSON'S VOICE
> I'm afraid so.
>
>   MARTIN
>   (clearing his throat)
> Is this a joke, sir?
>
>   FERGUSON
> No.
>
>   MARTIN
> But—you *can't*. Mr. Ferguson, you mustn't.

NEW ANGLE—MARTIN AND FERGUSON

Ferguson shakes his head.

>   FERGUSON
> I know how you feel, Martin, believe me I do.
> But I'm afraid there isn't any choice.
>
>   MARTIN
>   (genuinely stricken)
> I don't understand, I don't…
>
>   FERGUSON
>   (not wanting to tell him this)
> I have been offered a large sum for this property.
> Some people want to build a…supermarket here.

MARTIN
(the ultimate insult)
A *supermarket!*

FERGUSON
(rising)
Here, let me get you a drink. It will help settle you.

Ferguson goes to a cabinet, takes out a bottle and two glasses.

MARTIN
No…please. I—

Martin bites his lip; it is as if he's going to cry. Ferguson comes back, puts the bottle and the glasses on the desk, comes to him and puts a hand on his shoulder, CAMERA MOVING IN.

FERGUSON
(kindly)
When I first opened the museum…thirty years ago…I never dreamed I'd see this day. But the day is here, Martin…and we will just have to face it.

MARTIN
(stunned)
Thirty years!

FERGUSON
Oh, for heaven's sake, don't make it more difficult than it is. I hate this, Martin.
(beat)
We've been together a long time. You're the best employee a man could ever have.
(smiles)
The way you've run the Murderers' Row exhibit …why, I don't think you've ever missed a tour.

                    MARTIN
            I never did.

Ferguson pats his shoulders and moves off. Martin swallows, looks toward him, says anxiously:

                    MARTIN
            How many…more days?

FERGUSON

Taking his chair, not looking at him.

                    FERGUSON
            None. This was the last. They start wrecking
            the building next week.

Martin ENTERS FRAME to look at him with horror.

                    MARTIN
            No more tours? None at all?

                    FERGUSON
            I had to agree to it.

Martin is crushed, starts to turn away, then turns back.

                    MARTIN
            What about the figures?

                    FERGUSON
            I haven't decided yet.

Martin blinks his eyes several times, then has a happy thought.

                    MARTIN
            We'll open another museum. We'll move everything
            somewhere else. We don't have to give it up.

FERGUSON
(shaking his head)
I'm not as young as I was once. I need a rest.
Fanny and I—

MARTIN
(eagerly)
I'll do all the work. I mean it! You won't have
to do a thing, Mr. Ferguson. Not a thing.

Ferguson looks at him with a sad, little smile.

FERGUSON
I appreciate that, Martin, and I know you'd be
a great help, but…it would be foolish.

MARTIN
Foolish! Why?

FERGUSON
(getting up)
Let me show you something.

ANGLE PAST FILING CABINET IN F.G.

and TOWARD Ferguson who moves to it, opens a drawer and pulls out a file.

FERGUSON
We are passé, Martin. People aren't interested
in wax museums anymore.

ANGLE TO DESK

Ferguson returning to it, putting the file in front of Martin, who opens it, Ferguson taking his chair.

                    FERGUSON
    Look through it. It's all in there, our attendance
    figures, our gains, but mostly our losses. This
    last year has been the poorest of all. You'll also
    find a news story about the closing of the Grand
    Guignol. A sign of the times, the handwriting
    on the wall.

Ferguson opens the bottle, pours himself a drink.

                    FERGUSON
    Sure you won't have a drink?

                    MARTIN
                    (absorbed)
    No. No, thank you.

Ferguson takes a swallow, puts his glass down.

                    FERGUSON
    What did we offer them? A Room of Love
    where they could see the famous lovers of history
    …The Discovery Room where scientists were
    caught in motion at the moment of their greatest
    discoveries…The Presidents' Room…and all the
    others. But that isn't why people came here. That
    isn't why at all.

CAMERA MOVES IN as he takes another swallow, then says wryly:

                    FERGUSON
    Those rooms were only sidelights. What they
    really came to see was your Murderer's Row.
    We've always known that. But they have been
    coming in decreasing numbers, and do you
    know why? Because the outside world offers
    them fears we could never match. The ovens at
    Belsen and Dachau have ruined our chamber

of horrors. People are blasé, sophisticated; they think they have outgrown the need to be frightened. That isn't it. It's because they are afraid every day; they live in fear day in, day out. It's the world.
(beat)
No, Martin. It would be foolish to open another museum.

MARTIN

He will never give it up.

                MARTIN
Maybe it's the location, or the way we have the figures exhibited. Remember how people came after we worked out the Ripper's arm?

MARTIN AND FERGUSON

Ferguson shakes his head.

                FERGUSON
But that was years ago.

                MARTIN
An amusement park! We could put the figures in an amusement park.

                FERGUSON
I thought of that. I even made some inquiries today. But a wax museum is too static, they say. It doesn't *do* anything. They're simply not interested.

Martin's face is full of cooperation.

MARTIN
But if we don't open another museum—what's going to happen to the figures—to Landru and Hicks and the others?

FERGUSON
If I could sell them, I would. But there is no market for wax figures.

MARTIN
(horrible thought)
Mr. Ferguson—you're not thinking of *destroying* them!

FERGUSON
(some annoyance)
Martin, I tell you, I don't know *what* I'm going to do!

Martin, recovering from shock, draws himself to his full height, faces Ferguson squarely. He says grimly:

MARTIN
You're forgetting something.

FERGUSON
Forgetting something? What?

MARTIN
Come with me.

Martin moves off.

FERGUSON
Martin—

But Martin has moved through the door. Ferguson sighs, gets up to follow.

INT. MURDERERS' ROW—ANGLE TO DOOR

Martin strides into the room purposefully, Ferguson following more leisurely, but curious. CAMERA FOLLOWS them to the figure of Landru where Martin steps up to the platform, leaving Ferguson to look up at him. Martin indicates Landru. He is on home ground, familiar territory.

                  MARTIN
    Look at him, Mr. Ferguson. Look at his eyes.
    Don't you see the shy, frightened little choirboy
    he once was? Don't you see the bookkeeper who
    so longed for freedom?

Martin runs his hand along the cheek to the mouth.

                  MARTIN
    Even the cheek feels real—like flesh. And look
    at this mouth. Isn't it about to say something?
    Oh, Landru was an eloquent man, full of
    tenderness…and it's been caught here, in the
    mouth—

                  FERGUSON
               (exasperatedly)
    What are you trying to say, Martin?

Martin steps down and moves to Ferguson, CAMERA MOVING IN. Martin's eyes are full of fanatic gleaming.

                  MARTIN
    Mr. Ferguson, you seem to have forgotten that
    these figures are the work of the great Henry
    Guilmant—the only ones he ever created outside
    of Europe.

                  FERGUSON
    No, I haven't forgotten that.

                    MARTIN
            (turning to figures)
    There was genius in everything he did—so
    different from the crudeness of the other
    pieces. They're nothing—just so much candle
    wax. But these—it's as though they were alive.
            (then to Ferguson)
    Their flesh even has pores!

                    FERGUSON
    I know, but I'm afraid it doesn't make any
    difference to people anymore.

                    MARTIN
    Mr. Ferguson, it makes a difference to *me*.

Ferguson eyes him soberly, says with a trace of irritation:

                    FERGUSON
    Do you expect me to open another museum
    just because of that?

Martin turns away, walks to the figure of Hicks.

MED. SHOT—MARTIN

He inspects Hicks, then moves to Burke and Hare, CAMERA FOLLOWING. He is deep in thought, smooths the cloth on the figure being smothered. Then he turns toward Ferguson O.S.

                    MARTIN
    I want to buy them.

                    FERGUSON
    That's ridiculous.

Martin moves to the edge of the platform, jumps down and moves to Ferguson, CAMERA FOLLOWING.

MARTIN
(with anguish)
I don't think I could stand it if these figures were destroyed. It would be like—like losing five close friends.

The CAMERA MOVES so that Ferguson is in profile. He solemnly studies the figures, says softly:

FERGUSON
I won't destroy them, Martin. I give you my word. But where am I going to store them? You know how vulnerable they are to changes in temperature.

MARTIN
I could take them, Mr. Ferguson.

Ferguson turns to look at him, considering it.

FERGUSON
You? What would you do with them?

MARTIN
I wouldn't put them in an ugly warehouse, I'll tell you that.
(looks at figures)
They need constant caring for. Do you realize how much like children they are?

FERGUSON
Let's be practical, Martin. Where could you possibly keep them?

MARTIN
(turning to him)
In my basement. It's the perfect place.

                    FERGUSON
          For heaven's sake, what would Emma say to
          having the figures of five famous murderers in
          her basement?

                    MARTIN
          Oh, she'll understand. She always wanted
          children, so these would be our babies. You
          don't have to worry about Emma, Mr. Ferguson.
                    (looks to figures)
          I'll put in an air conditioner, that's what I'll do.
          And a heater for the colder days.

CAMERA moves up to, and in on, the Ripper's face. The eyes glisten darkly.

                    MARTIN (O.S.)
          I'll take care of them, just as I've always done…

                                                  DISSOLVE:

INT. MARTIN'S HOME—KITCHEN—FULL SHOT—DAY

A typical suburban home kitchen populated at the moment by Martin and EMMA SENESCU, about 45, a sweet-faced woman with an unhurried, unworried manner, pouring coffee for Martin, who sits at the table.

                    EMMA
          You haven't eaten your breakfast.

                    MARTIN
          I'm not hungry.
                    (looks at watch)
          They should have arrived by now.

He gets up and moves to a window. Emma sits down at her place to drink her coffee.

EMMA
They'll get here when they get here.
(beat)
How long will they be here?

MARTIN
(turning)
I have plans for opening my own museum, but I'll have to buy them from Mr. Ferguson first.
(looks at watch)
Maybe something happened to them. It's not like moving furniture, you know.
(paces floor)
They should have let me ride with them. What if they dropped one?

The SOUND of a moving van ENGINE slowing down is HEARD.

EXT. MARTIN'S HOME—WIDE ANGLE—DAY

A large moving van moves to a stop in front of the house.

ANGLE PAST REAR OF VAN IN F.G.

and TOWARD rear of house where Martin appears, striding quickly toward the van as he puts on a jacket.

ANGLE TO REAR OF VAN

Martin reaching it as two burly, uniformed van MEN get out and join him at the rear.

MARTIN
Are they all right?

The FIRST VAN MAN looks at the manifest as the SECOND VAN MAN prepares the rear of the van for unloading.

FIRST VAN MAN
You Martin Senescu?

MARTIN
(quickly)
Yes, yes.

FIRST VAN MAN
Everything's okay.

MARTIN
No bumps?

The van men exchange look-what-we've-got-here glances.

FIRST VAN MAN
No. No bumps.

The second van man lets down the tailgate, opens the rear doors where half a dozen solidly-constructed crates are situated, partly covered by padding and securely strapped to their positions. Both men jump into the van and start unstrapping the boxes.

FIRST VAN MAN
Where d'ya want 'em, Mr. Senescu?

MARTIN
Take them to the rear of the house, down into the basement…How long will it be?

FIRST VAN MAN
I dunno. An hour, maybe. You got to pay for an hour no matter how long it takes.

MARTIN
(nods, feels air)
It's getting warm.

FIRST VAN MAN
Huh?

MARTIN
I say it's getting warm. You see, they're delicate. They can't stand more than eighty degrees.

FIRST VAN MAN
Uh-huh.

They have unstrapped the first box and start it toward the gate.

MARTIN
Steady now...

The van men exchange glances again as they move the box.

DISSOLVE THROUGH TO:

INT. BASEMENT—MED. SHOT—VAN MEN AND MARTIN

The last box is being put into place beside the others, Martin hovering nervously about.

MARTIN
Easy...don't jiggle it...There.

Martin breathes a sigh of relief, as if he had done all the work himself. The bored first van man takes the manifest out of his pocket, hands it to Martin with a pencil.

FIRST VAN MAN
Sign here.

Martin signs, putting the paper on a box, hands the paper and pencil to the man as Emma ENTERS FRAME to look at the boxes. The men move off. Martin approaches a box and pats it affectionately.

                    MARTIN
          Landru's in this one. That one over there's
          Jack the Ripper.
                    (rubs his hands)
          Oh, Emma, it's going to be like opening
          Christmas presents.

                    EMMA
                    (dubiously)
          I didn't think they were so big.

                    MARTIN
          It's the boxes. The figures themselves aren't
          any bigger than we are.

Martin moves off, leaving Emma to look glumly at the boxes. He returns with a hammer.

                    MARTIN
          I'm going to have to be very careful with the
          uncrating.

There is an O.S. KNOCK. They look toward it.

ANGLE TO BASEMENT DOOR

An air-conditioner INSTALLATION MAN stands there in uniform.

                    INSTALLATION MAN
          Mr. Senescu?

BACK TO MARTIN AND EMMA

Martin pauses in the act of starting to work.

                    MARTIN
          Yes?

The installation man ENTERS FRAME.

> INSTALLATION MAN
> The movers said you were down here. Where do you want the air conditioner?

> MARTIN
> (pointing)
> It goes in that window there.

> INSTALLATION MAN
> Okay.

He moves off.

> EMMA
> You bought an air conditioner?

> MARTIN
> The figures can't stand heat. We had to have it.

> EMMA
> How much did it cost?

> MARTIN
> Don't you worry about it.

> EMMA
> But I *am* worrying about it.
> (looking around)
> Also I'm worrying about how I can do my washing down here with all this going on.

Martin stops his work to look at her in alarm.

> MARTIN
> You *can't* do it down here! The humidity—

                    EMMA
But it's got to be done! You don't have a decent
shirt to wear, and it's been a week since—

                    MARTIN
                    (firmly)
Go to the Laundromat! Go anywhere! But
leave me to my friends.

She stares at him in amazement, as we

                                        FADE OUT

FADE IN:

INT. BASEMENT—CLOSE SHOT—AIR CONDITIONER
LOUVERS—DAY

The force of blowing air flutters a ribbon tied to a louver. CAMERA DRAWS BACK, PANS to wax figures which have been set exactly as they were in the museum, with an improvised overhead spotlight on each one. CAMERA REACHES, HOLDS on Martin brushing Jack the Ripper's felt hat in his hands. He can't seem to get it right, keeps working it, inspecting it. Finally it meets his approval, he moves to Jack the Ripper, CAMERA FOLLOWING, placing the hat on his head, stepping back to observe the effect.

ANGLE UP STAIRS

The door at the top of the stairs opens and Emma starts down.

ANGLE PAST MARTIN IN F.G.

and TOWARD stairs. He still hasn't got the Ripper's hat the way he wants it, adjusts it again, takes a few swipes at it with the brush as Emma approaches. Her face somehow has lost the sweet repose of former days as she moves next to Martin and looks at the figure of the Ripper without love.

> EMMA
> You cleaned that hat last week.

> MARTIN
> Brushed it, you mean. But it's going to need cleaning and blocking before long.

Martin steps back and runs his eyes over all the figures, his face showing displeasure.

> MARTIN
> In fact, all their clothes could stand it. It's been almost a year.

Emma's face is strained.

> EMMA
> Martin…

> MARTIN
> The truth is they need *new* clothes. But the Ripper's the worst off. Part of his coat back's come undone and—

> EMMA
> *Martin!*

He turns to her in some annoyance.

> MARTIN
> What is it, dear?

> EMMA
> We are not buying them any clothes!

> MARTIN
> Oh, it isn't just *buying;* they've to be *tailored.* Their bodies—

                    EMMA
               (agony of frustration)
          I don't *care* about their bodies!

Martin stares at her in disbelief. She turns away.

ANOTHER ANGLE

Martin moving to her.

                    MARTIN
          Emma, you don't mean that!

                    EMMA
               (wretchedly)
          I do! Honestly, Martin, you're paying more
          attention to these—murderers—than you ever
          did to me.

                    MARTIN
          That's not true!

                    EMMA
               (turning to him)
          Then why are you down here every minute of
          the day and night?

                    MARTIN
          But don't you see? They're a trust. A sacred
          trust. These figures were made by Guilmant.
          They're masterpieces!

ANGLE TO EMMA

She is becoming genuinely disturbed. Glancing angrily at Hicks.

                    EMMA
          All right, so they're masterpieces. You told me

they'd be here for only a couple of days, and it's been ten weeks, do you realize that? I've been nice about it, Martin, you can't say I haven't. But how long am I going to be locked out of my own basement?

Martin takes her hand in his.

> MARTIN
> I'm sorry, dear. I didn't lie. I thought they'd be here only a little while—I really did—but I just can't find anybody who's willing to finance the museum.

> EMMA
> How can you find anyone if you spend all your time down here?

> MARTIN
> —I've phoned. But those people...
> (shakes his head angrily)
> They never even heard of Henry Guilmant. Can you imagine?

He has felt the letter she has in her hand, now takes it.

> MARTIN
> What's this?

> EMMA
> The electric bill. You'll see how much this air conditioner is costing us, running it day and night.

> MARTIN
> Well, you know how hot it's been, Emma.
> (inspects bill)
> This *is* high, isn't it...

                    EMMA
I'd like to know how we're going to go on paying it.
                    (suddenly contrite)
Oh, Martin, there's no more money in the bank!

He takes her in his arms, pats her head.

                    MARTIN
I know. But you mustn't worry. I—I'll think of something. There must be somebody somewhere...

                    EMMA
                (after a pause)
Mr. Ferguson.

SHOT—MARTIN

Moving away, disturbed by her suggestion.

                    MARTIN
No.

Emma ENTERS FRAME to talk over his shoulder.

                    EMMA
Why not? You've told me he loves them as much as you do. Besides, isn't it really up to him to take care of them?

He turns to her, his face set, determined.

                    MARTIN
Emma, I don't know anyone in the world I respect as much as I do Mr. Ferguson, yet I would never trust these figures to him. Don't

you see, I could never be sure they were being cared for *right*. I don't think I could sleep if—

                    EMMA
So we're stuck with them?

                    MARTIN
What do you mean we're stuck with them? Please! It's an honor—a privilege—

                    EMMA
For you maybe, but what about me? How do you think I feel? Every time I come down and see these—monstrosities, I just about get a heart attack. The way they stand there and stare at me, they're frightening.

                    MARTIN
                    (smiling)
But they're *supposed* to be frightening. I'll tell you something: you live with them as long as I have and you'll come to love them.

                    EMMA
                    (aghast)
Love them?

                    MARTIN
                    (matter of fact)
Yes.

He turns away, CAMERA FOLLOWING, moving to the Ripper, whom he regards fondly.

                    MARTIN
One day they cease to be strangers to you and you want to say good morning and ask them

how they spent the night. And when this happens,
Emma...
>(turns; beat)

Emma?

ANGLE UP STAIRS

Martin reaching the bottom of the stairs as the door closes.

>MARTIN
>Emma!

DISSOLVE:

INT. REAL ESTATE OFFICE—FULL SHOT—DAY

Typical trappings of a real estate office with its panels of keys, books of listings, photographs of homes and grandly eloquent descriptions thereof. DAVE SNYDER, a man of about 50, a little on the chubby side, and an inveterate cigar smoker, stands at the window looking out, being in PROFILE to us. Emma sits in a chair in front of his desk.

>EMMA
>...and today, when we got the electric bill, I
>realized we've been spending a fortune just
>to keep the basement cool for those dummies.

Dave turns, shakes his head, moves to the desk to sit on the edge of it and looks down at her.

>DAVE
>You should have told me about this before.

>EMMA
>I know, but I didn't want to bother you. I
>mean, you're so busy all of the time.

                    DAVE
I'm also your brother, remember?

                    EMMA
            (nods)
Oh, Dave, I shouldn't be complaining, not really. Martin isn't a bad person. It's just that…well…you know how he loved his job. It was such a shock losing it…

                    DAVE
            (firmly, but not unkindly)
Look—you want me to do something or not?

                    EMMA
            (after a beat)
Yes.

                    DAVE
Okay. I'll tell you—you may not believe this—I've always kind of liked the little guy…but what's happening now—with those things in the basement and all—it sounds like he could use a few hours with a head shrinker.

                    EMMA
Dave, you don't think he's—

                    DAVE
            (shrugs)
This is the way it happens.
            (reaches into his pocket and
                extracts his wallet)
I'll send you the name of a good psychiatrist. Meanwhile, take this.

                    EMMA
No, Dave—

                    DAVE
          (walks over and forces some bills
                  into her hand)
          Come on, one nut in the family is enough.
          You need money, I've got money—don't
          make a big deal out of it.

                    EMMA
Thank you.

NEW ANGLE—FAVORING EMMA

She is on the brink of despair, deeply ashamed of having to accept money from her brother.

                    EMMA
          If only one of those people he's been talking
          to would lend him enough to open his museum
          ...that would make everything all right.

                    DAVE
          Oh, Emma, nobody is going to put money
          into a crazy scheme like that.
                    (relighting cigar)
          Old Ferguson knew what he was doing when
          he sold out...and he was pretty smart to get
          Martin to take care of those dummies. It's not
          costing him anything. Pretty smart.

ANGLE TO DESK

Dave sits down and taps a pencil thoughtfully.

                    DAVE
          One way or another we're going to have to
          get Martin away from those things.
                    (beat)
          Has he got them all?

EMMA
(shaking her head)
Only a few.

DAVE
How come? Ferguson had 200 or 300, didn't he?

EMMA
Yes, but these are special. Some man in Europe made them.

DAVE
(smiling)
Well, they can't be too special if they're not worth anything.

EMMA
They are to him. It's the first time anything has come between us. I hate those murderers.

Dave gets up.

DAVE
Come on. Let's talk to him.

EMMA
No, Dave. It won't do any good.

DAVE
All right then, you talk to him. Not the way you have been—lay it on him. Tell him it's those stupid dummies or you.
(he walks over to her)
If that doesn't work there *is* something else.

EMMA
(a bit fearfully)
What?

                    DAVE
                  (smiling)
            Air conditioners break down, you know.

                    EMMA
                  (after a beat)
            I couldn't do a thing like that.

                    DAVE
            Couldn't you?

                                              DISSOLVE:

INT. MARTIN'S HOME—BASEMENT—CLOSE ON MARTIN

Running a comb through Landru's beard. An O.S. door OPENS and CLOSES. Footsteps upstairs. Martin stops his work, cocks his head to look up.

INT. KITCHEN—FULL SHOT—NIGHT

Emma has come in with a large package of groceries which she puts down on the table, starting to empty the sack and putting them away. The door to the basement opens and Martin comes in, Emma ignoring him, even when he moves to the table.

                    MARTIN
            Where have you been? You walked out while
            I was talking to you.

When Emma pays no attention, Martin follows her about.

                    MARTIN
            I know you're angry, but what can I do? I have
            to keep the figures in perfect condition…You
            can't let them go or they'll—
                  (sees groceries)
            I thought you said we didn't have any money.

                    EMMA
                 (facing him)
          I bought these with the money Dave gave me.

The reality of his domestic situation is thus brought home to Martin and he sinks to a chair in shock. Emma relents and goes to him.

EMMA AND MARTIN

Emma puts an arm around his shoulders.

                    EMMA
          Martin, we can't go on like this.

                    MARTIN
          I'll borrow some money from Mr. Ferguson.

                    EMMA
          Borrowing isn't going to help.

                    MARTIN
          All right, I'll mortgage the house.

                    EMMA
          That still isn't going to solve anything.

She pulls up a chair, CAMERA MOVING IN. She puts a hand over his, says tenderly:

                    EMMA
          Martin, nobody knows more than I do what
          those figures mean to you, but…

He draws back, eyes her hostilely.

                    MARTIN
          But what, Emma?…But *what?*

EMMA
(decisively)
But I simply won't have them in my house any longer.
(as he stares)
They're Mr. Ferguson's. Why shouldn't he take care of them for a while?
(beat)
Well, why shouldn't he?

MARTIN
(dully)
That's what you really think, isn't it. That's all they mean to you.

EMMA
Yes. I want you to call him tomorrow and tell him.
(pats his hand; smiles)
Once they're out of here, you'll be a different man. You'll see. You've lived with wax dummies so long, you've forgotten how to be a human being.

Suddenly he draws his hand back, slaps it down violently on the table, pushing his chair back, filled with fury, CAMERA DRAWING AWAY.

MARTIN
No!

CLOSE SHOT—MARTIN

Righteous indignation.

MARTIN
What kind of a friend do you think I am? I can't desert them now...not after all these years. They *need* me! They'd be lost without me!

EMMA

Seeing the enormity of what he is saying.

> EMMA
> Martin, they're not *alive!*
> (beat)
> They don't need *anybody!*

MARTIN

Eyes narrowing in suspicion.

> MARTIN
> Your brother put you up to this. Well, call him
> up and tell him it didn't work.

He gets up, moves to the basement door, goes through it, slamming it after him.

DISSOLVE:

THE BEDROOM—CLOSE ON CLOCK—NIGHT

Clock reads 1:20. CAMERA DRAWS BACK, PANS PAST Martin, asleep, to Emma, who lies with her eyes open. She turns her head, looks at Martin.

ANGLE PAST MARTIN IN F.G.

and TOWARD Emma. Satisfied Martin is asleep, she quietly slips out of bed, picks up her robe off a chair, moves off.

INT. KITCHEN—FULL SHOT—NIGHT

It is dark. The door to the other part of the house opens, Emma enters, turns on the light.

ANGLE TO DOOR TO BASEMENT

Emma reaches it, opens it, pauses to listen. No sound. She moves to go down.

BASEMENT—FULL SHOT—NIGHT

Black, then bright with light that casts hulking shadows as Emma turns on the lights at the top of the stairs. She moves down the stairs, stops at the bottom.

CLOSE SHOT—EMMA

She stares.

HER P.O.V.—THE FIGURES

In their spotlighted pools, looking sinister indeed.

BACK TO EMMA

Shuddering, turning away.

ANGLE TO AIR CONDITIONER

The ribbon ripples in the cool breeze, Emma glancing toward it as she moves by.

FUSE BOX

A dark corner. Emma reaches it, lifts the lid. Exposed are the fuses. She reaches up, hesitates. A shadow with the outstretched arm and knife of Jack the Ripper falls upon her and the wall. She whirls around.

KILLER'S P.O.V.—EMMA

Her eyes are filled with numbing horror as CAMERA ADVANCES. Utterly terrified, she shrinks back against the impenetrable wall, crying hoarsely:

                              EMMA
            Oh, my God!

                                                        CUT TO:

AIR CONDITIONER RIBBON

Blowing fitfully. A SCREAM is cut off quickly.

                                                       DISSOLVE:

INT. BEDROOM—CLOSE ON CLOCK—DAY

It reads 8:00. The alarm RINGS, a hand comes out, turns it off, CAMERA DRAWS BACK to show Martin sinking back on the pillow, blinking his eyes open to this new day. He turns to Emma's side of the bed, reacts with surprise, sits up.

ANGLE TO BED

Martin looking to where she should be, then around the room.

                             MARTIN
            Emma?

He yawns, slips out of bed, stretches, picks his robe from a chair, starts putting it on.

INT. KITCHEN—FULL SHOT—DAY

Martin comes in, looks around.

                             MARTIN
            Emma?

He scratches his head, looks to the basement door, starts for it.

ANGLE ON BASEMENT DOOR

Martin reaching it, opening it.

                    MARTIN
          Emma?
                    (beat)
          Emma, are you down here?

Giving a last look around the kitchen, he starts down.

INT. BASEMENT—ANGLE UP STAIRS

Martin comes down.

                    MARTIN
          Emma?

CLOSE ON MARTIN

Reaching the bottom. He looks toward the figures, then around the basement. When he spies Emma O.S., he reacts with horror.

HIS P.O.V.—EMMA

Slumped in the corner under the fuse box.

SHOT TOWARD MARTIN

Moving to the body, CAMERA PANNING with him. He kneels down.

                    MARTIN
          Emma…What's happened?

He would turn her over, but as he does so, his hand comes into contact with blood. CAMERA MOVES IN as he looks at the blood on his hand. Slowly he turns his head toward the figures.

PAN SHOT—THE FIGURES

Moving slowly, left to right, Hicks, Burke and Hare, Landru, Jack the Ripper. CAMERA HOLDS, then ZOOMS IN on the knife.

ANOTHER ANGLE—JACK THE RIPPER

Martin reaching the figure, dazed and numbed, staring at the knife in revulsive disbelief. Martin reaches out, touches the blood-smeared knife, backs away a step, looks up at Jack the Ripper's eyes in horror.

FADE OUT

FADE IN:

INT. MARTIN'S HOUSE—BASEMENT—CLOSE SHOT—SPADE—DAY

It digs into the ground. CAMERA DRAWS BACK to show Martin using the spade. He has excavated an area of the basement floor the size of a grave, is just about finished. He pauses in his work, gets out a handkerchief, dabs at his face, looks O.S.

> MARTIN
> I don't like to put you here like this, Emma, but what can I do?

He puts the handkerchief back, commences digging again, depositing the dirt on the cement beside the grave.

> MARTIN
> I know I should report it to the police—I *want* to report it—but who would believe me if I told them you were killed by Jack the Ripper?
> (a slightly maniacal giggle)
> …You can see that, can't you?

He pauses, leans on the spade, looks to the figures.

                    MARTIN
    Besides, if I were to go to prison, which would
    surely happen, who would take care of the
    figures?
                    (beat)
    No. It is better this way.

He digs a little more.

ANOTHER ANGLE—CLOSER

Martin pausing, looking to Emma's corpse.

                    MARTIN
    They didn't like you, you know. You said
    some very unkind things about them. And
    they heard you.
                    (beat)
    You just didn't understand. You have to be
    careful with Jack, he has such a temper. He
    attacks without warning.
                    (looks at figures)
    I should have told you more about Jack.
    I should have warned you.

MED. SHOT—MARTIN

Turning to Emma again.

                    MARTIN
    Poor Emma. But it's too late to tell her
    anything now.

He sighs and commences his digging again.

                                    DISSOLVE THROUGH TO:

INT. BASEMENT—CLOSE ON MARTIN

Working with a trowel on fresh cement on the floor. The pile of dirt is gone; only cement tools remain adjacent to what is now Emma's grave. Martin regards the cement critically, makes a few final flourishes with the trowel.

                        MARTIN
            There. It's the best I can do.

CAMERA DRAWS BACK as he stands and inspects the job. A loud KNOCK on the basement door jars Martin to the very marrow.

                    GAS MAN'S VOICE
            Gas man!

ANGLE TO BASEMENT DOOR

It opens and a middle-aged GAS METER MAN in uniform and cap, with his ever-present record book, comes in, closing the door behind him. He grins as he starts across the floor.

                      GAS MAN
            Hi, there, Mr. Senescu!
                (mispronouncing it Seness-que)

MED. SHOT—MARTIN

The gas man reaches him as a dismayed Martin stands mute with the trowel still in his hands. The man takes no note of Martin's reaction, looks down at the fresh cement.

                      GAS MAN
            Doing a little patching, I see. Floor must have
            been pretty bad, huh?

                      MARTIN
            Yes. It—it was cracking.

                    GAS MAN
    Well, I had to do the same thing in my
    basement...That's the way it is with these old
    houses, you know.

                    MARTIN
    Yes.

The gas man turns to move on to the meter, stops, startled at seeing the wax figures.

                    GAS MAN
    Holy mackerel!

MARTIN AND GAS MAN

Gas man shaking his head.

                    GAS MAN
    Phew! For a minute there...Where'd you ever
    get anything like that?

                    MARTIN
    They belong to Mr. Ferguson. I'm keeping
    them for him. They used to be in his museum,
    but it's closed.

                    GAS MAN
    Boy, they're the most realistic things I ever saw.
            (steps back; grinning)
    You sure they ain't alive?

                    MARTIN
    Not altogether.

                    GAS MAN
            (peering at figures)
    Well, they could fool me.

He moves off.

ANGLE TO GAS METER

Gas man reaching it, shining his light at the dials, making his entries in the book.

> GAS MAN
> Sure'd be a fine thing to have come Halloween. Something like that in the basement and you'd really throw a scare into people.

He turns and starts off.

ANGLE TO FIGURES

Gas man reaches them before Martin does, the gas man staring at them with admiration.

> GAS MAN
> Man, oh man, even up close they—What's that?

> MARTIN
> (in alarm)
> What?

JACK THE RIPPER

The gas man moves to the outstretched arm, touches the blade, Martin moving into position to press the floor button. The gas man is so situated that his throat would be cut by the knife.

INSERT

Martin's foot only an inch from the button.

BACK TO SCENE

The gas man shakes his head in amazement.

                    GAS MAN
          Whoever made these up thought of everything.
          Even put blood on the knife. Pretty good.

With a final look at the figures, he turns.

                    GAS MAN
          Well, I've gotta go, but I want to tell you
          you've got quite a layout here.
                    (afterthought)
          Tell me something, don't they give you the
          creeps…I mean, being down here in the
          basement and all?

                    MARTIN
          Not when you know them as well as I do.

Gas man laughs, starts off, Martin following, CAMERA MOVING with them.

                    GAS MAN
                (laughing a bit nervously)
          You're a card, Mr. Senescu, you know that?
          Wait'll I tell the wife about this!

ANGLE TO BASEMENT DOOR

Martin opens it, gas man hesitating.

                    GAS MAN
          Hey, you think it would be all right if I brought
          her over to look at those things?

                    MARTIN
          No!—I mean, we're going to be gone for awhile.

                        GAS MAN
            Tomorrow?

                        MARTIN
            Days. We don't know when we'll be back.

                        GAS MAN
                    (getting the message)
            Oh…Well, I'll see you next month, then. So
            long.

                        MARTIN
            Goodbye.

Gas man goes out, Martin closes the door with relief and locks it, then turns to move off.

JACK THE RIPPER

Martin reaching the figure, standing before it, frowning.

                        MARTIN
            I'm surprised at you, Jack, truly surprised.

He moves to the figure, removes the blade from the outstretched hand.

                        MARTIN
            How did you ever manage all those murders
            without being caught by Scotland Yard?

He starts off with the blade.

ANGLE TO SINK

Martin reaching it, turning on the water, washing and scraping the blade to get rid of the tell-tale blood.

                    MARTIN
          Any killer knows you can't leave blood on the
          murder weapon. It's a—and I don't mean to
          make a joke, Jack—it's a dead giveaway.
                    (holds up knife)
          There. Good as new.

He starts off.

JACK THE RIPPER

Martin reaching him, reinserting the knife.

                    MARTIN
          Now you behave yourself. I don't want to
          go through anything like this again.

A KNOCK on the basement door startles him.

                    DAVE'S VOICE
          Emma?...Martin?...You down there?

CLOSE SHOT—MARTIN

Alarmed, undecided what to do, his eyes darting to the fresh grave O.S. The KNOCK is LOUDER and Martin wets his lips.

                    DAVE'S VOICE
          Martin! If you're down there, open up!

ANGLE TO BASEMENT DOOR

Martin moving to it, thinking furiously as the KNOCKING continues. His hand reaches for the lock, draws back.

                    DAVE'S VOICE
          Martin!

                    MARTIN
            All right, all right. I'm here.

                    DAVE'S VOICE
            Open the door.

                    MARTIN
            No.

                    DAVE'S VOICE
            Why not?

                    MARTIN
            I can't...I—I've got a lot of material piled
            up in front of it. I'll come upstairs. The back
            door.

Martin starts away.

INT. KITCHEN—ANGLE TO BASEMENT DOOR

Steps coming up, the door opens, Martin comes through. He closes the door, runs his hand along the molding until he finds the key, locks the basement door.

                    DAVE'S VOICE
                (outside the back door)
            You there, Martin?

                    MARTIN
            Coming.

He moves to the door to the outside, CAMERA FOLLOWING. He unlocks it, Dave coming in.

                    DAVE
            Wow, you keep this place locked up like Fort
            Knox or something. What's the big idea?

MARTIN
We always keep the doors locked.

ANGLE TO TABLE

Dave reaching it, Martin behind him.

DAVE
Where's Emma?

MARTIN
She isn't here.

DAVE
(taking a chair)
Maybe it's just as well.

MARTIN
Why? What do you want?

Dave doesn't answer, takes out a cigar, proceeds to unwrap it, looks around.

DAVE
Got an ash tray somewhere?

MARTIN
I'll get a saucer.

He gets one, Dave lighting the cigar, Martin remaining standing.

DAVE
Sit down, Martin.

MARTIN
To tell you the truth, Dave, I'm rather busy right now.

                    DAVE
                (heavy sarcasm)
I'll bet.

                    MARTIN
If you'll just tell me what you want—

                    DAVE
Come on, sit down.

Martin sits, CAMERA MOVING IN. Dave looks at him.

                    DAVE
Emma came to see me yesterday.

                    MARTIN
I know. She told me about it.

                    DAVE
                (some surprise)
She did, huh? Well, that'll make it easier. Where'd she go, by the way?

                    MARTIN
She—she took a trip.

                    DAVE
A trip? Where?

                    MARTIN
To see my sister.

                    DAVE
Oh.
                (frowns)
You two have an argument?

MARTIN
Everything's settled now.

ANOTHER ANGLE

Dave considers how to proceed in view of this development.

DAVE
I'm glad to hear that. But—well, she was pretty upset when she talked to me.

MARTIN
I know.

DAVE
You've got to admit you didn't treat her square when you brought those dummies here and Kept her out of her own basement.

MARTIN
That's been changed.

DAVE
(relieved)
Well, now I guess I had you pegged wrong. You got rid of them?

MARTIN
Yes.

DAVE
(with a chuckle)
Must have been pretty hot last night, huh?

MARTIN
Hot?

                    DAVE
                (another laugh)
          Yeah, pretty hot for a bunch of wax dummies.

He eyes Martin, expecting some kind of reaction, but Martin's answering look is a vacant one. Dave, suddenly ill at ease, brings out a match and relights his cigar. He blows out the match, cocks his head.

                    DAVE
          What's that humming noise?

                    MARTIN
          I don't hear anything.

                    DAVE
          Sounds to me like it's coming from the
          basement.
                (narrows eyes)
          Hey, that's the air conditioner. What are you
          trying to hand me?

ANGLE PAST TABLE TOWARD DOOR

Dave getting up and striding to the door, Martin rising. Dave tries the door, turns to Martin in surprise.

                    DAVE
          This door's locked.

                    MARTIN
          I told you we always keep the doors locked.

Dave glowers at him, moves to him, CAMERA MOVING IN.

                    DAVE
          Why should the air conditioner be going if
          you got rid of the wax figures?

MARTIN
(shrugging)
I was cleaning up down there, that's all. I wanted it cool.

DAVE
But you just came up from down there and you locked the door behind you. Now why—

MARTIN
Locking doors is just a habit of mine.

DAVE
I don't think so. I think you locked it because you don't want me to go down there. You'd better open up.

MARTIN
Are you threatening me in my own house?

CLOSE SHOT—DAVE

He regards Martin for a long moment, chewing on his cigar, clearly angry but trying to think it through.

DAVE
You didn't get rid of them things at all…and this sister of yours…How come Emma never mentioned her before?…Where does she live?

SHOT—MARTIN—DOOR TO OUTSIDE IN B.G.

He sighs, takes his chair at the table, turns his back on Dave.

MARTIN
Look, I'm tired of answering questions and I've had a busy day. I'll thank you to leave.

Dave ENTERS FRAME to look down at Martin, a crafty, superior look blossoming on his face. Elaborately:

                    DAVE
     Okay, I guess I can take a hint. I'll be leaving.

Martin does not answer. He is very obviously frightened. Dave starts for the door to the backyard, pauses, turns.

                    DAVE
                 (casually)
     You have Emma call when she gets back, hear?

Martin nods. Dave goes out, closes the door. Immediately Martin gets up, goes to the door and locks it.

EXT. MARTIN'S HOUSE—FULL SHOT—REAR OF HOUSE—DAY

Dave coming down the steps, moving to go to the driveway to the front, pausing to look back at the door, then moving close to the house toward the basement door.

BASEMENT DOOR

Dave reaches it, tries it. It won't open. He looks around, moves off.

BASEMENT WINDOW

Dave reaches it, bends down, shades his eyes, looks in.

REVERSE ANGLE

The window is dirty and curtained; Dave can barely be seen through it.

BACK TO DAVE

Rummaging through his pockets. He gets out a pocket knife, inserts it along the frame, jimmies the lock. The window swings inward.

INT. BASEMENT—ANGLE TO WINDOW

Dave peering in, deciding to come in, lowering himself to the floor, gently closing the window. He stands in the dim light of the basement, looks around.

HIS P.O.V.—THE BASEMENT

The dimly-seen wax figures, the walls, the stairs, the air conditioner.

DAVE

Striking a match, cupping it in his hands, starting forward.

HICKS

Dave reaching him. Hicks is perhaps even more malevolent in the half-light of the flickering match.

DAVE

The match burns his finger, Dave mutters, waves it out. He strikes another one, moves on.

PAN SHOT—THE OTHERS

Illuminated one by one by the eerie effulgence of the single match.

DAVE AND JACK THE RIPPER

Dave shakes out the match, lights another, looks at Jack the Ripper briefly, then turns, takes a few steps, CAMERA FOLLOWING. Dave's foot strikes something that skitters mechanically along the floor. He bends down, picks up the trowel with fresh cement on it. He studies it, then looks O.S.

BASEMENT FLOOR

The grave.

ANGLE TO GRAVE

Dave lights a fresh match, gets down on his haunches, pushes his finger into the wet cement.

CLOSE SHOT—DAVE

The enormity of what he is thinking is written on his face. His match blows out. He whirls.

CUT TO:

HICKS' AX

Held in two hands, ready to descend.

CUT TO:

KILLER'S P.O.V.—DAVE

Surprise and terror on Dave's face as he sinks back. He SCREAMS.

CUT TO:

THE TROWEL

Hitting the floor and rattling along it for a few feet.

DISSOLVE:

INT. KITCHEN—ANGLE TO TABLE—NIGHT

Martin finishing the last of his meal, drinking his coffee, then getting up and taking dishes to the sink.

SINK

Martin unhurriedly rinsing them, drying his hands on a towel. He turns, moves off.

ANGLE TO BASEMENT DOOR

Martin reaches the door, completely relaxed. He opens the door, turns out the kitchen lights, starts down the stairs.

ANGLE UP STAIRS

Martin turns on the lights, starts down. Before he is halfway down, he spies the body of Dave O.S., reacts with horror.

                        MARTIN
     Dave!

HIS P.O.V.—DAVE

A crumpled heap on the floor.

BACK TO MARTIN

He moves down the stairs, dazed by what he sees.

ANGLE TO DAVE

as Martin reaches him, kneels down, reaches out to touch him, draws back in alarm.

PAN SHOT

Shooting through rear of figures toward Martin as he slowly turns his head to look at them.

MARTIN

Staring.

HIS P.O.V.—HICKS

The upraised ax.

ANGLE TO HICKS

as Martin moves to him to stare up at the ax covered with blood.

> MARTIN
> Hicks, how could you?
> (beat)
> You didn't even *know* him!

FADE OUT

FADE IN:

INT. MARTIN'S HOUSE—BASEMENT—ANGLE TO BED—DAY

Martin propped up by pillows, dozing in a rollaway bed he has set up in one corner of the basement, a shelf of books to one side and a lamp burning over his head; the book he was reading when he fell asleep lies open on his chest. A KNOCK is HEARD at the basement door. Martin does not stir.

EXT. MARTIN'S HOUSE—ANGLE TO BASEMENT DOOR—DAY

Ferguson stands there, raises his hand, knocks again.

> FERGUSON
> Martin?

When there is no answer, he moves from the door.

ANGLE TO WINDOW

The same window Dave used. Ferguson reaches it, crouches, endeavors to peer through it. He knocks on it.

                    FERGUSON
            Martin!

INT. BASEMENT—CLOSE ON MARTIN

The KNOCK on the basement window is repeated.

                    FERGUSON'S VOICE
            Martin!

Martin's eyes open sluggishly, he blinks sleepily, then sits up. He looks O.S. toward the window. The KNOCK again.

                    FERGUSON'S VOICE
            Martin! Are you down there?

Martin gets off the bed.

ANGLE TO WINDOW

Martin reaches it, opens it, sees Ferguson, reacts.

                    MARTIN
            Mr. Ferguson!

                    FERGUSON
            For heaven's sake, Martin, I've been trying
            to raise you for half an hour. Don't you
            answer your door anymore?

                    MARTIN
            I was asleep. I'm glad you came, though.

                    FERGUSON
            Aren't you going to open the door?

                    MARTIN
            Oh...yes. Just a moment.

He lets the window fall in place, starts off.

ANGLE TO BASEMENT DOOR

Martin reaching it, opening it, Ferguson coming in.

> MARTIN
> I'm sorry I didn't hear you, Mr. Ferguson, but with the air conditioner and everything, I can't hear anything upstairs.

Ferguson looks around.

> FERGUSON
> Well, it's nice and cool down here.
> (sees figures)
> Ah, there they are.

> MARTIN
> (proudly)
> Yes, they're still here…and in perfect condition.

They start for them.

ANGLE TO FIGURES

Martin and Ferguson reaching them.

> FERGUSON
> I would have come two days ago when you called, but things hadn't been settled yet.
> (beat)
> I must say, Martin, you've kept them up well.

> MARTIN
> I've done my best; it's been a pleasure. We get along fine.
> (beaming)

You just don't know what a relief it is to see
you. The company has been threatening to cut
off the electricity because I haven't paid the
bill—and without electricity for the air
conditioner, think what would happen to the
figures!

FERGUSON

Well, you don't have to worry about that anymore.

MARTIN

I'm glad to hear it, Mr. Ferguson. I knew I
could count on you.

ANGLE PAST JACK THE RIPPER IN F.G.

and TOWARD Martin and Ferguson as Martin moves to the Ripper.

MARTIN

But the trouble with the electric company isn't
all…Look at this.

Martin reaches up, takes the backside of the Ripper's coat to show it to
Ferguson.

MARTIN

It needs to be fixed badly; the threads are just
falling out.
      (gravely)
In fact, they all need new clothes.
      (beat)
I've been thinking maybe it's too humid down
here after all.

FERGUSON

We won't have to worry about that either.
Have you heard of the Marchand Museum in
Brussels, Martin?

                    MARTIN
         No, I can't say that I have, Mr. Ferguson.

Martin starts off.

ANGLE TO LANDRU

Martin reaching him, Ferguson behind him. Martin indicates a place on the sleeve.

                    MARTIN
         I was going to have Emma repair this little rip
         in the sleeve, but there were so many things to
         do…

                    FERGUSON
         By the way, how *is* Emma?

                    MARTIN
         Oh, fine. She's off on a visit right now.

                    FERGUSON
         You have a remarkable wife, Martin. There
         aren't many women who would put up with
         an exhibit like this in the basement.

                    MARTIN
         She never complains.

Ferguson turns away, puzzledly eyes the bed in the corner.

                    FERGUSON
         Have you been sleeping down here?

                    MARTIN
         Yes. That reminds me of something.

He starts off.

ANGLE TO BED

Martin reaching it, followed by Ferguson.

>   MARTIN
> I brought all my books down here, and I came
> across an item in this one just before I fell asleep.

He picks up the book on the bed.

>   FERGUSON
> Martin, there's something you ought to know.

>   MARTIN
>   (ignoring it)
> Remember how excited we used to get when
> we'd find out something new about the figures?
> Well, I found this book in the closet—I even
> forgot I had it. And it's got a letter in it written
> by Landru himself.

>   FERGUSON
> Martin—

MARTIN AND FERGUSON

Martin moistening his lips.

>   MARTIN
> Listen.
>   (reading)
> "But for you, whose very walk is beautiful,
> whose sweet eyes and smile make a just claim
> to happiness…whither am I bound, my dear
> little friend, under your tender leadership?"
>   (beat; looks up)
> Isn't that touching?…To think that Landru
> could write things like that!

                    FERGUSON
                    (nodding)
          It's the one he wrote to Fernande Segret.

                    MARTIN
          You know it then!

                    FERGUSON
          He also strangled her, as he did all the others.

                    MARTIN
          But the letter proves he wasn't just a callous
          murderer!

Ferguson sighs, eyes him gravely, looks as if to answer, then looks back to the bed.

                    FERGUSON
          Tell me, does Emma approve of your sleeping
          down here like this?

                    MARTIN
          She hasn't objected.

                    FERGUSON
                    (with admiration)
          I repeat that Emma is a most unusual woman.
                    (beat)
          But why should you *want* to stay down here?

ANGLE TOWARD BED

Martin walking into CLOSE SHOT as he looks at the figures.

                    MARTIN
          I felt it best to keep an eye on them, Mr.
          Ferguson. Some strange things have been
          happening.

Ferguson joins him to SHARE FRAME.

> FERGUSON
> Strange things?

> MARTIN
> Yes.
> (beat)
> You see, they haven't exactly been behaving themselves.

> FERGUSON
> Oh, come now.

> MARTIN
> (turning to him)
> It's true, Mr. Ferguson. I swear it's true. You've no idea what they've been up to.

ANOTHER ANGLE

as Ferguson looks toward the figures, then turns back to Martin to look at him solemnly.

> FERGUSON
> Martin, you've been so close to these figures for the past three months, you're beginning to imagine things about them.

> MARTIN
> Oh, no. It wasn't my imagination. Not at all.

> FERGUSON
> Well, that's neither here nor there. The point is, you won't have to take care of them much longer.

> MARTIN
> But I *want* to take care of them!

SHOT—FERGUSON

He has to tell him, but he doesn't like it.

> FERGUSON
> I know you do, and as I've said, I appreciate what you've done. But I have sold the figures to the Marchand Museum.

SHOT—MARTIN

As if struck by a body blow.

> MARTIN
> You—sold them?

FERGUSON

Moving to Martin.

> FERGUSON
> Yes, and for what I'm getting, there will be a substantial reward to you for all the years you've cared for them.

> MARTIN
> But my museum! I was going to buy them and open my own exhibit!

> FERGUSON
> (gently)
> You know you could never do that.

> MARTIN
> (despairingly)
> You can't do it! Tell them you have another buyer! I'll get the money somehow! Please, Mr. Ferguson!

Martin casts an anguished glance toward the figures.

> MARTIN
> They're all I have left in the world!

Ferguson puts his arm around Martin's shoulder, starts off.

ANGLE TO FIGURES

as Ferguson moves Martin to them, Martin's face full of gloom.

> FERGUSON
> Martin, everything changes. There was a time when there was a place in this country for a wax museum, a place where people could go to indulge their curiosity or their lust for sensation.

MARTIN AND FERGUSON

Ferguson, still with his arm around Martin, looking at the figures.

> FERGUSON
> But that time is past. Time has moved on for us, and other things have replaced the bloodlike red wax in the museum. People can see it happening now; they can see it in the boxing arena, on the race courses, on the playing field, on the freeways. There is no longer any need for our specialty.

Ferguson smiles, takes his arm away and turns Martin to him.

> FERGUSON
> I thought that, with the closing of the Grand Guignol things were must the same in Europe. But Marchand's is—fortunately for us—*expanding.* They were delighted to make an

offer, and the transaction was consummated only this morning.

>   MARTIN
>   (woebegone)
>   But what am I going to do without the figures?
>   Mr. Ferguson, I—I'd die without them!

>   FERGUSON
>   Nonsense, Martin. You only *think* you would.
>   You'll get over it.
>   (beat)
>   Now why don't you prepare us a cup of tea or
>   something while I take some measurements.
>   The Marchand people want some specifications
>   I can't provide.

Martin nods glumly.

>   MARTIN
>   All right, Mr. Ferguson.

He moves off. Ferguson takes out a tape measure and a notebook and prepares to measure the figures.

ANGLE UP STAIRS

Martin reaches them, starts up.

FERGUSON

Taking the measure of Hicks by holding the tape measure with his foot and running it to the top of the ax Hicks holds over his head. He releases the measure, which is of the collapsible type and runs back into the container. Ferguson grunts, makes a notation.

>   FERGUSON
>   Six feet, one inch.

He looks to the next exhibit, CAMERA MOVING with him to Burke and Hare, which he measures lengthwise along the floor from Burke's heel to Hare's. Again he makes a notation.

                FERGUSON
      Hmm. Eight feet. I didn't think it was that wide.
                  (beat)
  No matter.

He proceeds to measure the height of Hare.

                FERGUSON
      Five feet, ten inches.

The CAMERA MOVES IN on Ferguson's face as he makes the entry. Suddenly Landru's waxed cord whips down over his head and is wound about his throat, Ferguson unable to speak, dropping everything, clawing at the cord in terror.
                                      CUT TO:

INT. KITCHEN—TEA KETTLE—DAY

It commences a SHRILL WHISTLE. The CAMERA DRAWS BACK as Martin ENTERS FRAME to lift it from the stove.

ANGLE PAST TABLE IN F.G.

and TOWARD stove. Two cups and saucers have been arranged on the table. Martin moves from the stove with the teakettle, fills the cups, puts the teakettle back, returns to pick up the two cups and saucers.

ANGLE TO DOOR TO BASEMENT

Martin reaching the door, which has been left open, and starting down the stairs.

INT. BASEMENT—ANGLE UP STAIRS

Martin descending with the tea.

> MARTIN
> I forgot whether you used sugar or cream, Mr. Ferguson. If you want it, I'll go back up.

He is so involved with keeping the cups from spilling that it isn't until he gets to the bottom of the stairs that his eyes move to where Ferguson is supposed to be. He reacts, drops the cups and saucers which crash on the cement floor.

> MARTIN
> (horrified whisper)
> Mr. Ferguson!

ANGLE TO FERGUSON

as Martin reaches him, horror-struck. He shakes him, takes his hand, then sees the waxed cord, which he lifts easily from Ferguson's throat, CAMERA MOVING IN as Martin eyes it with loathing. His head slowly turns to the figures, and his eyes are no longer filled with love for them.

> MARTIN
> Landru!... *You* did this!

MARTIN

Rising from floor, his mouth set in a grim line as he looks to the figures, the waxed cord still in his hands, blinking his eyes as he regards them. With sudden decision he turns away.

ANGLE TO WORK BENCH

Martin reaching it. He looks up on the pegboard, reaches for a hammer, hesitates, reaches instead for the ax, takes it down, turns, his face full of determination.

ANGLE TO FIGURES

as Martin walks up to them, the ax held in his hand loosely at his side. His entire manner toward the figures has changed; he clenches his teeth in anger.

>   MARTIN
> Hicks…Burke and Hare—oh, I know you didn't have any part of this, but you didn't *stop* it—and you, Landru, *especially* you…and Jack.
>   (beat)
> You've gone too far.

CLOSE ON MARTIN

There is resignation, hurt and anger in him.

>   MARTIN
> I gave you all the best years I had. You wanted for nothing. I washed you, cleaned your clothes, bought you new ones…It was always the right temperature for you because I made it so…I defended your deeds before thousands who came to see you…And when Mr. Ferguson sold the museum, who was it that spoke up for you, who was it that wanted you?
>   (beat)
> I was the best friend you ever had…and now—what have you done for me?

ANGLE PAST FERGUSON'S BODY TOWARD MARTIN

Who turns to it.

>   MARTIN
> You have murdered Mr. Ferguson. The only man who was my friend. My best friend.

ANGLE PAST FIGURES TOWARD MARTIN

He turns to them.

>   MARTIN
> The books were right. I see that now. You're
> monsters, do you hear that? Heartless monsters
> all the way through, every last one of you!
>   (beat)
> And for that I'm going to punish you. I shall
> cut you all up into little pieces, turn up the heat,
> and let you melt into pools of wax. And it will
> be no more than you deserve.

MARTIN

He looks from one to the other.

>   MARTIN
> Now, who shall be first?
>   (looks at Landru)
> You, Landru. Because it was you who
> murdered Mr. Ferguson.

He starts forward.

FULL SHOT—THE FIGURES

Martin advancing on Landru. Suddenly the figures come to life, HICKS lowers the ax, BURKE and HARE turn from their victim, JACK THE RIPPER turns to Martin, and LANDRU reaches up to take Martin's ax-wielding arm. Martin stops mid-stride.

CLOSE SHOT—MARTIN

Now he is terror-stricken as his eyes dart from one to the other. He backs away.

HIS P.O.V.—LANDRU

Advancing on him, his face full of hate.

> LANDRU
> No...It was not I who garroted your friend,
> Martin Senescu.
> > (points finger)
> It was *you!*

MARTIN

Backing away, lips working, eyes wide in fear.

> MARTIN
> No! You! You killed him while I was upstairs
> making tea!

JACK THE RIPPER

Shakes his head, advancing.

> JACK THE RIPPER
> No, Martin Senescu, it was you; it was *always*
> you. You took my blade and murdered your wife!

MARTIN

Shock-filled.

> MARTIN
> You killed her while I was asleep!

HICKS

Advancing, eyes full of loathing.

> HICKS
> It was you who used my ax to kill your wife's
> brother!

MARTIN

Shaking his head.

                      MARTIN
           No! No! *You* killed him!

OVER-SHOULDER SHOT—MARTIN—TOWARD FIGURES

As they advance, glowering at him, converging on him.

                      MARTIN
          You all lie! You're the murderers!

                      BURKE
             Not so, Martin Senescu!

                      HARE
            (with crushing finality)
     You are the murderer. You killed them all.

Martin stumbles, falls out of CAMERA RANGE. The figures leap after him. We HEAR Martin's SCREAM.

                                          DISSOLVE:

EXT. BUILDING—MED. SHOT—SIGN

Reading: MARCHAND'S WAX MUSEUM.

                             DISSOLVE THROUGH TO:

INT. MUSEUM—MURDERERS' ROW—DAY

We see Hicks, Burke and Hare, Landru and Jack the Ripper behind the roped-off area just as they were in Ferguson's Museum. In front of the ropes, addressing a crowd of PATRONS, is a uniformed GUIDE, an older man somehow reminiscent of Martin Senescu, but obviously not he.

                    GUIDE
          Hicks was hanged at Bedloe's Island in
          America on July 13, 1860.
                    (starts to move)
          And now we come to the man who only recently
          became one of the most famous of all…

The crowd starts to move along with him.

MED. SHOT—MARTIN

Martin's wax figure is shown in the position of digging with a spade. The crowd moves in to view him, CAMERA MOVING IN TO A CLOSE-UP as the guide speaks.

                    GUIDE
          …Martin Lombard Senescu, a remarkable and
          certainly versatile murderer…Who knows what
          thoughts went through his mind as he dug the
          graves for his wife, Emma, whom he killed with
          a knife, and his wife's brother, David, whose
          skull was split with an ax? Who can even hazard
          a guess why he killed them at all? And I ask you
          why should he have committed his third murder,
          that of his best friend and employer of thirty
          years, Ernest Ferguson. We can only guess what
          fierce devils tortured his soul and drove him to
          his destiny…

Living Doll

Original Airdate: November 1, 1963

LIVING DOLL

FADE IN:

EXT. STREATOR HOUSE—FULL SHOT—DAY

An attractive two-story residence in a tract. Well-kept lawn, carefully cultivated flower beds, manicured bushes. A fairly new car comes down the street and stops.

FRONT OF HOUSE

ANNABELLE STREATOR, a housewife of about thirty, calmly attractive, gets out from behind the wheel with several small packages. CHRISTIE STREATOR, about six, gets out on the other side with a large box, runs around to join her mother. They approach the CAMERA; when they are in MED. CLOSE SHOT, Annabelle puts her hand on Christie's shoulder, looks down to her as Christie looks up.

                    ANNABELLE
                    (pleasantly)
     Now remember, honey, I want you to run
     upstairs with your present.

> CHRISTIE
> Can't Daddy see it?

> ANNABELLE
> Not right away. Do you understand?

> CHRISTIE
> Yes, Mommy.

They start for the door.

INT. HOUSE—STUDY—MED. SHOT—ERICH STREATOR

A comfortable, small study. ERICH STREATOR, about thirty-five, sits at a small desk, frowning. Before him is a large checkbook and the desk is covered with bills. His sleeves are rolled up, his collar open, his tie loosened. We hear the O.S. SOUND of a door OPENING, CLOSING. He looks up.

ANGLE TO DOOR

Erich moving to the door as Annabelle and Christie reach it. Christie hesitates, looking at her father.

> ERICH
> Hi. What did you buy?

> ANNABELLE
> Nothing much.
> (to Christie)
> Go on, Christie.

Christie gives her mother a look of despair before she turns to start off.

> ERICH
> Wait a minute, Christie. What have you got there?

                    ANNABELLE
            It's just a doll, Erich.

Christie waits for the outcome.

                      ERICH
            She doesn't *need* another doll.

                    ANNABELLE
            It's one she's had her eye on for months.

                      ERICH
            I thought we agreed—

Annabelle makes a pained face, brushes past him.

ANOTHER ANGLE

Annabelle moving to the studio couch to put down her purchases.

                    ANNABELLE
                    (to Christie)
            You might as well open it.

Christie moves in with Erich; she is beaming, can't get the lid off the box quickly enough.

                     CHRISTIE
            She's *alive,* Daddy, and her name's Talky Tina.

She withdraws an ugly doll about half her size.

                      ERICH
                     (annoyed)
            For heaven's sake, Annabelle, a doll like that
            costs—

                    ANNABELLE
          I put it on the account.

                    CHRISTIE
          Tina does everything.

CLOSE SHOT—CHRISTIE

Christie fascinatedly winds a key in the back of the doll.

                    CHRISTIE
          She moves and walks and she can even talk
          and I just love her already.

The doll writhes in ghastly slow motion. Christie pulls a ring on the side of the doll's neck, lets it go.

                    DOLL
          My name is Talky Tina and I love you very
          much.

Christie giggles, looks toward her O.S. parents for their reaction, pulling the ring again.

TWO SHOT—ANNABELLE AND ERICH

Annabelle watches the O.S. with amusement. Erich is grim.

                    DOLL'S VOICE
          My name is Talky Tina and I love you very
          much.

                    ERICH
          All right. How much did it cost?

                    ANNABELLE
          I told you I—

                    ERICH
I know. You charged it. *How much did it cost?*

                  ANNABELLE
                  (reticently)
          Twenty-three ninety-five.

                    ERICH
                   (aghast)
          Twenty-three ninety-five?

                 DOLL'S VOICE
    My name is Talky Tina and I love you very
    much.

                  ANNABELLE
          But dear, a doll like that—

ANGLE TO CHRISTIE

Absorbedly pulling the ring again.

                 ERICH'S VOICE
                  (in misery)
        That's all we need, a doll that talks.

                     DOLL
    My name is Talky Tina and I love you very
    much.

Erich ENTERS FRAME.

                    ERICH
                   (sharply)
        Will you please shut that thing off!

Christie, wrenched from her fascination, turns frightened eyes to her father, sees his wrath. She drops the doll to the studio couch, starts to run from the room, crying.

FULL SHOT—STUDY

Christie running out, Annabelle darting a withering look to Erich before starting after her.

                  ANNABELLE
    Christie...

ANGLE TO DOLL

It writhes on the studio couch, its eyes closed, the CAMERA MOVING IN. The doll slows down, stops, and when CAMERA is in CLOSE SHOT, the eyes jerk wide open.

                SERLING'S VOICE
    Talky Tina, the doll that does everything, a
    lifelike creation of plastic and springs and
    painted smile.

SHOT—SERLING

                    SERLING
    To Erich Streator, she is a most unwelcome
    addition to his household—but without her,
    he'd never enter the Twilight Zone.

                                          FADE OUT

FADE IN:

INT. STREATOR HOUSE—CHRISTIE'S BEDROOM—DAY

Annabelle sits on Christie's bed, drying Christie's tears with a handkerchief. Erich stands nearby looking neutral.

                    ANNABELLE
          It's all right, honey. Daddy says we can keep
          the doll.

Erich makes a wry face. Christie looks to him to see if her mother is telling the truth.

CLOSE SHOT—ERICH

Trying to smile.

                    ERICH
          I promise, Christie.

BACK TO SCENE

                    ANNABELLE
                    (to Christie)
     See?

Erich sighs, moves to leave room.

                    ERICH
          Man is helpless in the face of a female alliance.
                    (beat)
          I'll be downstairs.

He goes out. Annabelle smiles at Christie.

ANGLE PAST STUDY DOOR

Erich comes down the stairs, moves to the study door.

INT. STUDY—FULL SHOT

Erich coming in, going to the desk, moving some papers around, then looking toward the doll.

ANGLE TO STUDIO COUCH

Erich moving to look down at the doll darkly. He picks it up, winds the key. The doll writhes grotesquely. He looks at it distastefully.

CLOSE ON ERICH

He pulls the ring, lets it go.

                DOLL
My name is Talky Tina and I don't think I like you.

Erich reacts, blinks, lets the doll run down. When it stops writhing, he pulls the ring again.

                DOLL
My name is Talky Tina and I think I could even hate you.

Erich flares, throws the doll across the room. It hits the wall with a dull THUMP.

CLOSE ON DOLL

It writhes slowly, stops, its eyes on Erich O.S.

                DOLL
My name is Talky Tina…and you'll be sorry.

ANGLE PAST ERICH IN F.G.

and TOWARD door. He stares at the O.S. doll as Annabelle comes in to stand beside him, looking first at him and then at the O.S. doll.

              ANNABELLE
Erich.

She starts for the doll.

ANGLE TO DOLL

Annabelle picking up the doll, turning to Erich vexedly as he ENTERS FRAME with residual anger.

> ANNABELLE
> *Why*, Erich?

> ERICH
> I don't like what it says.

> ANNABELLE
> You didn't have to *throw* it.

> ERICH
> It has quite a vocabulary.
>   (taking doll, pulling ring)
> Listen.

> DOLL
> My name is Talky Tina and I love you very much.

> ERICH
> (staring at doll)
> That's not what it said a minute ago.

Annabelle crosses into the room, turns now, faces Erich.

> ANNABELLE
> (beat)
> Erich, I don't know how much more of this I can take….

> ERICH
> Oh? And exactly what is it you're taking?

                    ANNABELLE
                    (sincerely)
          Your anger toward Christie. I know you're
          Having a difficult time adjusting to her, but I
          can't let you treat her like a stray animal.
          She's my daughter, Erich. I love her.

                    ERICH
                    (with sarcasm)
          You love her. But I don't love her. I'm only
          her stepfather. I'm incapable of loving children
          because I can't have any of my own. That's
          what you're saying, isn't it, Annabelle?

                    ANNABELLE
          Oh, no, Erich. Believe me, it's not. You could
          love Christie, I know you could, if you'd only
          give yourself half a chance.

                    ERICH
                    (bitterly)
          Good. Then I'm not the cold, cruel ogre
          Mommy and Daughter think I am. I can't tell
          you how much I appreciate your faith in me.

                    ANNABELLE
                    (comes to him warmly)
          Erich, *please* give us a chance; Christie *and* me.
          I know you got more than you bargained for
          when you married me. Two for the price of one,
          wasn't it? But we'll do anything to make you
          happy. Both of us.

                    CHRISTIE'S VOICE
          Daddy!

ANGLE TO DOOR

Christie coming in, CAMERA FOLLOWING HER to Annabelle and Erich. When she puts up her hands for the doll, Erich draws it away.

                      ERICH
        Not just now.

                    CHRISTIE
               (face clouding)
    But Daddy—

He gets down on his haunches to face her.

                    ERICH
      Christie, honey, listen…

                  ANNABELLE
     Erich, you promised.

Reluctantly, he gives her the doll. As she moves off, she pulls the ring.

ANGLE TO DOOR

Christie carrying the doll out in such a way that when it opens its eyes it seems to stare at Erich.

                    DOLL
   My name is Talky Tina and I love you very
   much.

CLOSE SHOT—ERICH

Puzzled, not sure if his senses have deceived him.

                                          DISSOLVE:

INT. DINING ROOM—ANGLE TO TABLE

Annabelle, Christie and Erich seated eating their dinner, the doll in an old high chair. Christie pretends to feed the doll as a mother would.

                    CHRISTIE
          Be a good girl, Tina, eat your supper.

                    ERICH
          Eat your own supper, Christie.

They eat in silence.

CLOSE SHOT—ERICH

He eats, glowers across the table.

P.O.V. SHOT—THE DOLL

It stares back insolently.

GROUP—FAVORING ERICH

He is annoyed with the doll's unblinking gaze.

                    ERICH
          Christie, isn't there some way to close her
          eyes?

                    CHRISTIE
          But Tina's eating, Daddy.

                    ERICH
          (after a pause)
          I don't see why you had to bring her to the
          table.

TWO SHOT—ERICH AND ANNABELLE

Erich turning to Annabelle.

                    ERICH
        I've never seen such hideous eyes.

                    ANNABELLE
        She's just a doll.
                (beat)
        And Christie needs her.

Erich looks at her sharply.

                    ERICH
        Lacking a brother or sister, is that what you
        mean?

                    ANNABELLE
                (stiffly)
        I didn't say that.

                    ERICH
        But it's why you bought it, so I'd have a
        reminder.

Annabelle gives him a cold look, gets up, stacks her dishes.

                    ANNABELLE
                (stonily)
        It hadn't occurred to me…but if that's what
        you think—

The front door chime SOUNDS. Annabelle turns, moves off.

ANGLE TO TABLE

Annabelle leaving the room, Erich finishing his meal, Christie winding the doll. O.S. a door OPENS.

                    LINDA'S VOICE
        Can Christie play?

Christie gets off her chair. Annabelle comes to the doorway.

> ANNABELLE
> It's Linda. Are you through with your dinner?

> CHRISTIE
> Yes, Mommy...Can I take Tina?

> ANNABELLE
> Not outside. You can show her to Linda later.

Christie goes. Annabelle ignores Erich, starts to clear the table. Erich lights a cigarette, watches her. The O.S. door OPENS and CLOSES. The doll slowly writhes in the high chair. Annabelle goes out to the kitchen.

SHOT—DOLL

Slowing down, blinking its eyes.

> DOLL
> My name is Talky Tina and I'm beginning to hate you.

SHOT—ERICH

Reacting, glowering, then controlling himself, smiling.

> ERICH
> My name is Erich Streator and I think I'm going to get rid of you.

SHOT—DOLL

Wide-open stare.

> DOLL
> You wouldn't dare.

TWO SHOT—ERICH AND DOLL

                    ERICH
        Wouldn't I?

Getting up he moves over to the doll, picks it up, CAMERA MOVING IN.

                    DOLL
        Annabelle would hate you...Christie would
        hate you...and I would hate you.

ANGLE TO DOOR TO KITCHEN

Annabelle comes in, CAMERA FOLLOWING HER to the table where she picks up more dishes. She glances to Erich with the doll, hesitates. Erich smiles, nods to the doll.

                    ERICH
        Just seeing how it works.

Annabelle turns away, picks up the dishes, goes out.

SHOT—ERICH

Amusedly examining the doll, probing here and there, looking sat all the joints. He pulls on a leg, twisting it a little.

                    DOLL
        Oh!

                    ERICH
        So you have feelings?

                    DOLL
        Doesn't everyone?

                    ERICH
                (wide grin)
            Then I could hurt you.

                    DOLL
        Not really. But I could hurt you.

                    ERICH
                (with a laugh)
            Threats from a doll!

ANGLE PAST ERICH

To the door of the kitchen, which opens, Annabelle coming in, stopping, looking around.

                    ANNABELLE
            Who were you talking to?

He moves to her with the doll, still smiling. He hands it to her.

                    ERICH
            Here. The game's over.

She takes the doll, stares at him innocently.

                    ANNABELLE
            Game?

                    ERICH
        Oh! Come on, now. How dense do you think I am?

                    ANNABELLE
        I wish I knew what you were talking about.

ANGLE PAST ANNABELLE AND ERICH

and TOWARD table. He moves to the table to get his coffee cup.

                    ERICH
          I admit I haven't kept up with the times. I
          didn't know they were putting walkie-talkies
          in dolls.

                    ANNABELLE
          Walkie-talkies?

He joins her with his coffee cup.

                    ERICH
          Come off it, Annabelle. Didn't you think I'd
          catch on? All that stuff about hating me—and
          that last bit about feelings.
                    (mimicking doll)
          Doesn't everyone?
                    (normal voice)
          You should be in comedy.
                    (moving off)
          I need more coffee.

Annabelle stares at him, bewildered. She turns at the SOUND of the front door OPENING, CLOSING.

ANGLE TO DINING ROOM DOORWAY

Christie coming in with LINDA, a girl about her age. CAMERA FOLLOWING THEM to Annabelle.

                    CHRISTIE
          Linda wants to see Tina.

Annabelle hands her the doll.

                    ANNABELLE
                    (absently)
          Here you are, dear.

Annabelle moves worriedly toward and through the door to the kitchen as CAMERA MOVES IN on Christie and Linda. Christie winds the doll.

                      CHRISTIE
        Watch.

Linda watches wide-eyed as the doll writhes. Christie pulls the ring.

                      DOLL
        My name is Talky Tina and I love you very much.

Both girls giggle with pleasure. They start off.

                      LINDA
        Let me do it.

ANGLE PAST TABLE IN F.G.

and TOWARD kitchen door. Erich coming through it with his coffee. Annabelle behind him.

                      ANNABELLE
        You can think whatever you want to, but it's not true.

                      ERICH
        Go ahead, pretend, but I know you've got a
        microphone around here somewhere.
                (almost desperately)
        You *must* have.

                      ANNABELLE
        The doll only says one thing.

                      ERICH
        I notice it never talks when you're in the
        room with me.

Annabelle, seeing his certainty, sinks to a chair and stares at him, disturbed.

                    ANNABELLE
            You're really serious.

He grimaces extravagantly, sips his coffee.

                    ANNABELLE
            You really mean it.

                    ERICH
                    (harshly)
            Of course I mean it.
                        (beat)
            So tell me.

                    ANNABELLE
                (almost a wail)
            But there's nothing to tell!

SHOT—ERICH

Getting angrily to his feet, pushing his chair back.

                    ERICH
            All right, *don't* tell me. Keep your secret.

He stomps out of the room, CAMERA FOLLOWING.

EXT. HOUSE—CHRISTIE AND LINDA

The door to the house is in the B.G. They sit on the front steps with the doll, Linda winding it. The door opens, Erich coming out in an agitated state, lighting a cigarette, seeing them. The doll makes its movements. Linda pulls the ring. Erich looks at them calculatingly, turns to look down the street.

                    DOLL
            My name is Talky Tina and I love you very
            much.

Erich joins them.

> ERICH
> How would you like some ice cream?

> CHRISTIE
> (jumping up)
> Linda too?

> ERICH
> Sure.
> (digs for change)
> There's the truck down the street.

He gives them some money. They move to start off, Christie with the doll.

> ERICH
> Leave the doll here, Christie.

She relinquishes the doll; they move off quickly. Erich watches them go, then looks down at the doll with distaste and distrust. He looks toward the window and then back to the doll before starting off.

ANGLE TO REAR OF HOUSE

Erich ENTERING FRAME and moving toward a garbage can, the doll under his arm.

SHOT—ERICH

At the garbage can, reaching for the lid.

> DOLL
> Ooh—are you going to be sorry!

Erich hesitates but for a moment. Then, with a victorious smile, he tosses the doll in, clamps the lid back on, snorts contemptuously, moves off.

DISSOLVE TO:

INT. STUDY—FULL SHOT—NIGHT

Erich seated in a comfortable chair reading a newspaper. Christie runs to him from the doorway.

> CHRISTIE
> Where's Tina, Daddy?

MED. TWO SHOT—ERICH AND CHRISTIE

Erich stiffens but does not look up from the paper.

> ERICH
> I wouldn't know.

> CHRISTIE
> You had her, Daddy.

> ERICH
> Go ask your mother.

ANGLE TO DOOR

Annabelle standing there, aloof.

> ANNABELLE
> She's already asked me.

SHOT—ERICH

Looking up.

> ERICH
> (an accusation)
> And what did you tell her?

CAMERA DRAWS BACK to INCLUDE Christie and Annabelle, who joins them.

>   ANNABELLE
>   That you'd know where she is.

>   CHRISTIE
>   Where is she, Daddy?

Erich goes back to his newspaper.

>   ERICH
>   (coldly)
>   If your mother can't tell you, then neither can I.

SHOT—ANNABELLE

Disturbed by his attitude, but controlling herself, turning to Christie, putting her arm around her.

>   ANNABELLE
>   Tina must be somewhere about, Christie.
>   Let's look for her.

They start off.

SHOT—ERICH

Waiting until they are out of the room, then lowering the paper to look after them, his face a study.

CLOSE SHOT—TELEPHONE

It RINGS. The CAMERA DRAWS BACK to INCLUDE Erich, who puts down the paper, getting up and moving to the phone, picking it up.

>   ERICH
>   Hello?

Erich reacts as he hears:

> DOLL'S VOICE
> (filtered)
> My name is Talky Tina and I'm going to kill you.

> ERICH
> (after a pause)
> Who is this?...Annabelle?

He clicks the receiver several times.

> ERICH
> Hello? Hello?

He slams the phone down in anger, abruptly starts off.

EXT. HOUSE—ANGLE TO BACK DOOR—NIGHT

The door opens, Erich coming out, CAMERA FOLLOWING HIM to the garbage can.

CLOSE ON GARBAGE CAN

Erich takes the lid off, leaning the garbage can TOWARD CAMERA so that we can see, with him, that it is empty. CAMERA MOVES IN on his face as he lets the garbage can rock back to its original position, sets the lid back on, then turns to stare O.S. with an expression of uneasiness.

FADE OUT

FADE IN:

INT. HOUSE—DINING ROOM—ANGLE TO DOOR

Erich comes through the door to the kitchen in a rage.

                        ERICH
        Annabelle!

He crosses to the doorway to the hall, CAMERA FOLLOWING.

ANGLE DOWN HALLWAY TOWARD STAIRS

Erich ENTERING FRAME.

                        ERICH
        Annabelle!

Annabelle appears on the stairs, looking at him in surprise as she descends. Erich stops at the study door.

MED. SHOT—ERICH

Seething with anger.

                        ERICH
        Where is she?

Annabelle joins him.

                        ANNABELLE
        She's still looking.

                        ERICH
        I don't mean Christie.

                        ANNABELLE
        We haven't found the doll, if that's what you
        mean.

                        ERICH
        That's exactly what I mean. You knew I put it
        in the garbage can and—

                    ANNABELLE
                    (cutting in)
         You *what?*

                    ERICH
         —It isn't there now.

SHOT—ANNABELLE

Distressed.

                    ANNABELLE
         Oh, Erich, how could you?

INT. STUDY—ANGLE TO DOOR

Turning away from her, coming in, trying to control himself. She follows him.

                    ERICH
         I'm tired of all this walkie-talkie nonsense. A
         joke's a joke, Annabelle, but you've carried it
         too far.

                    ANNABELLE
         I?

                    ERICH
         Please, don't make it any worse.

The CAMERA FOLLOWS him to the desk where he drops to his chair, furiously lights a cigarette. Annabelle joins him, looking down at him uneasily.

                    ANNABELLE
                    (softly)
         Erich, I didn't touch the doll. I haven't even
         seen it since dinner.

                              (beat)
                    I swear it.

Erich considers it. He frowns.

                              ERICH
                    You're telling the truth? You didn't take it?

                              ANNABELLE
                    I didn't take it…But I think it's dreadful,
                    your putting it there.

                              ERICH
                    Then who…?

                              ANNABELLE
                    I should have returned it.

                              ERICH
                              (almost to himself)
                    Somebody must have come along and…

He looks to her sharply, his face darkening.

                              ERICH
                    The phone call.

                              ANNABELLE
                    What phone call?

                              ERICH
                    You were on the extension. You said—

                              ANNABELLE
                              (bewildered)
                    What are you talking about?

                    ERICH
            Didn't you talk about it?

                    ANNABELLE
                    (exasperated)
            Do *what?*

ANOTHER ANGLE

Erich looking at her for a long moment, then getting up, for the first time considering that Annabelle might be telling the truth. He paces about thoughtfully, Annabelle watching him concernedly.

                    ERICH
            No, of course it couldn't have been you. How
            could you have made the telephone ring—

He stops to face her, saying thoughtfully:

                    ERICH
            There *are* ways, of course. But…

                    ANNABELLE
                    (completely at sea)
            Erich—

CLOSE SHOT—ERICH

Thinking it out as he talks.

                    ERICH
            The phone rang. I answered it. The doll's
            voice was loud and clear. It said, 'My name
            is Talky Tina and I'm going to kill you.'

MED. SHOT—ANNABELLE

Taken aback.

ANNABELLE
What?

ERICH
(joining her)
That's what it said.
(seeing her disbelief)
Would I lie?

ANNABELLE
(after a pause; worried)
Oh, Erich, I don't know what to say.

ERICH
Well, the doll's gone. Maybe things can settle down around here now.

ANNABELLE
Don't forget Christie.

ERICH
What about her?

ANNABELLE
How can you it explain it to her?

ERICH
We'll buy her another one. I'll talk to her. Is she upstairs?

ANNABELLE
Yes.

Erich starts off.

ANGLE DOWN UPSTAIRS HALLWAY

Erich reaching the top of the stairs.

                    ERICH

           Christie?

INT. CHRISTIE'S BEDROOM—ANGLE ON DOOR

Erich reaches the door, looks in. He reacts, moves into CLOSE SHOT, looks down in shock.

P.O.V. SHOT—CHRISTIE

Asleep in her bed, the doll at her side, Christie's arm draped over her. The doll's eyes are closed.

SHOT—ERICH

Frowning, recovering.

                    ERICH
                   (softly)
           Christie?

TIGHT TWO SHOT—CHRISTIE AND DOLL

The doll's eyes flip open, stares at Erich O.S.

                    DOLL
           I told you you'd be sorry.

ANGLE TO BED

Erich standing over it, flushing with new anger. He reaches over Christie to take the doll.

                    DOLL
           Christie! Christie!

                    ERICH
           Shut up!

He succeeds in removing the doll.

> DOLL
> Wake up, Christie!

Christie wakes up, sees Erich's wild state and the doll.

> CHRISTIE
> Daddy!

> ERICH
> Go back to sleep, Christie.

> CHRISTIE
> I want my Tina!

> ERICH
> I'm going to—borrow Tina for a while.

Christie senses his real intent, jerks to a sitting position.

> CHRISTIE
> Tina belongs to me!

Erich starts from the bed. Christie's face tenses; she starts to cry.

> CHRISTIE
> (a sob)
> Daddy!

ANGLE TO DOOR

Erich reaching it just as Annabelle starts in. The SOUND of Christie CRYING is HEARD.

> ANNABELLE
> What's happening?

ERICH
I found the doll in her bed.

ANGLE TO BED

Annabelle moving to it, taking Christie in her arms.

ANNABELLE
It's all right, Christie. It's all right, honey.

CHRISTIE
I want Tina!

Annabelle casts a helpless look to Erich.

ANNABELLE
Erich…

SHOT—ERICH

He makes up his mind.

ERICH
No.

He turns and leaves the room.

TWO SHOT—CHRISTIE AND ANNABELLE

Annabelle holding the sobbing Christie.

ANNABELLE
There, there…

LOWER HALLWAY—ANGLE TO STAIRS

Erich coming down purposefully, grimly, the doll under his arm.

EXT. HOUSE—ANGLE TO BACK DOOR—NIGHT

Erich comes out, turns on the patio lights, the area blossoming brightly. CAMERA FOLLOWS him to the hooded charcoal broiler.

CLOSE ON BROILER

Erich unceremoniously dumps the doll among the ashes of previous charcoal fires. He reaches into his pocket for a lighter, brings it out, lights it. As soon as it comes near the doll's dress, it blows out. He tries it again. It will not light, though he flicks it several times.

ANGLE TO BACK DOOR

It opens, Annabelle coming out.

> ANNABELLE
> Erich?

MED. SHOT—ERICH AT THE BROILER

Erich reaches to a nearby ledge shelf, glancing to Annabelle, who joins him. He takes down a box of wooden matches.

> ANNABELLE
> What are you doing?

> ERICH
> What I have to.

He strikes a match, holds the doll clothes out to light them.

> ANNABELLE
> Erich—*No!*

She moves to the broiler to pick up the doll. Erich stops her.

ERICH

Leave it alone!

Annabele draws back, frightened by his zeal. Erich strikes another match. Annabelle turns away, moves off. Erich stands with the match, turning to watch her.

P.O.V. SHOT—ANNABELLE

She moves into the house without a backward glance.

AT THE BROILER

The match burns his finger. He drops it, turns back, strikes another match, holding out the clothes. They will not burn. He frowns as he lights another match to try to ignite the doll. He still cannot make the doll's dress burn. He stares at the doll for a moment, then throws the box of matches back on the shelf, looks around angrily, spies a rack of knives, forks and other barbecue utensils. He takes the largest knife, moves to the doll, tests the cutting edge of the knife. Satisfied, he sets the knife edge at the doll's throat, commences sawing. Nothing happens. The knife will not cut. He lets out his breath in frustration, glares at the doll hatefully, looks toward the garbage can, picks up the doll roughly.

ANGLE TO BACK DOOR

Erich moving to a trash barrel beside the back door, picking out newspapers, a potato sack and rope. He takes this and a paper carton beside the barrel, moves off.

ANGLE TO PICNIC TABLE

Erich puts the doll on the picnic table, lays out the newspapers, wraps the doll quickly, inserts this into the sack, shoves the sack in the box, ties the rope around it, starts off with it.

ANGLE TO GARBAGE CAN

Erich reaches the garbage can, drops the box in, clamps down the lid, looks around, finds an unused concrete stepping stone, with effort manages to get this on top of the lid. He stands back to observe his work.

> ERICH
> Now, let's see you get out of that.

He turns and moves to the back door, CAMERA FOLLOWING.

INT. BEDROOM—FULL SHOT

Annabelle is emptying drawers of her belongings, putting them in a suitcase on the bed. A closet door stands open; some of the clothes are on the bed. Her movements are angry, determined.

ANGLE TO DOOR

Erich appears there, looks in, surprised.

> ERICH
> What are you doing?

He moves to her side, CAMERA FOLLOWING.

> ANNABELLE
> What does it look like?

> ERICH
> But why?

> ANNABELLE
> (pausing to look at him coldly)
> Why? How could I live with you after what you've done?

> ERICH
> I had to do it—the doll—

                    ANNABELLE
            You had to do it—to get revenge…just because
            I spent some of your precious money!

She turns away, but he reaches for her, turns her around.

                        ERICH
                      (flaring)
            Now listen, Annabelle. That doll talked to me.
            It said things no doll should say.
                      (beat)
            Don't you see? I *had* to get rid of it.

                    ANNABELLE
            You've become a stranger to me, Erich. A sick,
            neurotic stranger. And Christie—I don't want
            her hurt.

                        ERICH
            You're taking Christie?

                    ANNABELLE
            Of course.
                      (beat)
            And you'd better see a good psychiatrist.

She resumes her packing.

SHOT—ERICH

Sinking slowly to the bed, the implication clear, considering it miserably.

                        ERICH
                  (almost to himself)
            I *couldn't* have imagined it.

ANGLE TO BED

Annabelle continuing her packing.

                    ANNABELLE
          Tell him you burned a doll.

                    ERICH
                    (gloomily)
          I didn't burn it.

                    ANNABELLE
                    (hesitating)
          What *did* you do with it?

Erich gets up to face her, CAMERA MOVING IN.

                    ERICH
          I'll bring the doll in. I'll give it to Christie.
          Will that solve things?

                    ANNABELLE
          It would be a start, Erich.

He turns, goes. Annabelle looks after him worriedly, sits on the bed.

EXT. HOUSE—ANGLE TO DOOR—NIGHT

Erich coming out, turning on the patio lights.

ANGLE TO GARBAGE CAN

Erich reaches it, lifts off the stone, removes the lid, takes out the box, slips off the rope, takes out the sack, depositing the box in the garbage can, then the sack, then the papers.

ANGLE TO BACK DOOR

Erich carries the doll in, turns off the lights.

ANGLE DOWN UPSTAIRS HALLWAY

Erich reaching the top of the stairs.

ANGLE PAST CHRISTIE AND ANNABELLE IN F.G.

and TOWARD door. Christie, here face tear-stained, is in bed in her pajamas, Annabelle beside her. Erich appears in the doorway with the doll. He starts toward them.

                CHRISTIE
       Tina! Tina!

ANGLE TO BED

Christie holding out her arms for the doll, happy. Erich gives it to her, Annabelle watching. Christie embraces the doll.

                CHRISTIE
       Oh, Tina!

Annabelle gets up, moves to Erich's side, he takes her hand. They both look down at Christie, then at each other, smiling.

                            DISSOLVE:

INT. BEDROOM—FULL SHOT—NIGHT

Annabelle in one twin bed, Erich in the other. The room is lighted by what comes through the windows. Abruptly, Erich sits up.

ANGLE TO BEDS

Annabelle awakening, sitting up, looking to Erich, who sits in a listening attitude.

                    ANNABELLE
                     (softly)
         What is it?

                      ERICH
         I heard something.

He moves to swing his legs out, stands. Annabelle starts to get up.

                      ERICH
         No. You stay here.

She sinks back, frightened. Erich moves off.

ANGLE DOWN HALLWAY

Erich moving out into the hallway, advancing TOWARD CAMERA stealthily. He stops at Christie's door.

INT. CHRISTIE'S BEDROOM—CLOSE ON DOOR

It opens. Erich peers in. His eyes widen in surprise.

P.O.V. SHOT—CHRISTIE

The doll is not beside her.

FULL SHOT—BEDROOM

Erich moving quietly in, looking around. He turns, starts out.

ANGLE DOWN HALLWAY

Erich coming out, closing the door softly. He starts TOWARD CAMERA.

CLOSE TRACKING SHOT—ERICH

Moving down the hall, turning to the stairs, stopping.

P.O.V. SHOT—DOWNSTAIRS CORRIDOR

Illuminated by a night light. It is empty.

MED. CLOSE SHOT—ERICH

Starting down the stairs.

ERICH'S FEET

Tripping over the doll.

ANGLE DOWN STAIRS

Erich falling down them, uttering a harsh scream.

AT THE BOTTOM OF THE STAIRS

Erich falling INTO FRAME.

FAST PAN SHOT—THE DOLL

It follows him down the stairs, falling to lie beside him.

CLOSE SHOT—ERICH'S FACE

Agonized, stunned, staring.

P.O.V. SHOT—DOLL'S FACE

On the floor beside him, eyes open, mocking.

ANGLE TO ERICH

He slumps in death, his eyes closing. Annabelle's O.S. SCREAM is HEARD. Lights go on.

ANGLE TO STAIRS

Annabelle rushing down.

> ANNABELLE
> Erich!

ANGLE PAST ERICH'S BODY IN F.G.

And TOWARD the approaching Annabelle, who kneels down, her marrow freezing as she looks at him.

> ANNABELLE
> (a gasp)
> Erich.

She reaches out a trembling hand to him, draws it back in shock when she hears:

> DOLL'S VOICE
> My name is Talky Tina…

She looks toward the doll.

CLOSE SHOT—DOLL'S FACE

> DOLL
> …and you'd better be nice to me.

CLOSE SHOT—ANNABELLE

Eyes widening in fear, drawing back in horror, shaking her head as CAMERA DRAWS BACK to INCLUDE doll.

SERLING'S VOICE
Of course we all know that dolls can't talk...
Not really. And they certainly can't commit
murder. That is, unless they happen to be
from the Twilight Zone.

FADE OUT

Queen of the Nile

Original Airdate: March 6, 1964

QUEEN OF THE NILE

FADE IN:

EXT. BEL AIR MANSION—FULL SHOT—DAY

A resplendent residence, sumptuous and ornate, with a curving driveway from the ironwork gates up to the long veranda. The lawns are immaculate, the bushes manicured to perfection. A picturebook home. A sports car enters the driveway, slowly moves to the veranda.

MED. SHOT—VERANDA

The car comes to a stop, but the driver, JORDAN HERRICK, does not get out.

CLOSE SHOT—JORDAN

He is a man in his early thirties, handsome, virile, and exuding alertness. As he looks up and down the veranda, he shakes his head in disbelief, chuckles softly, starts to get out.

ANGLE TO DOORWAY

Two large heavy doors with a gold escutcheon of the scarabaeid beetle in the center of each; they are knockers. Jordan moves to the door, eyes the gold beetles wryly, lifts one, lets it fall. It THUDS LOUDLY.

CLOSE ON DOOR

Jordan waiting. It is opened by a MAID who eyes him hostilely. Instantly Jordan's face blossoms into smiling congeniality.

> JORDAN
> I'm Jordan Herrick. I have an appointment
> With Miss Morris.

> MAID
> (without change)
> Come in, please.

INT. MANSION—FULL SHOT—HALL—DAY

Plush, with curving staircase, chandeliers, mirrors and deep pile carpeting. Jordan comes in, the maid closing the door behind him. She starts off.

> MAID
> This way.

Impressed, but not overcome, Jordan moves to follow.

INT. LIVING ROOM—FULL SHOT—DAY

Elegant, lavishly furnished, with the scarab theme in evidence (but not overdone). The maid enters, Jordan following. She turns to him.

> MAID
> I will tell Miss Morris you're here.

She goes.

CLOSE SHOT—JORDAN

Looking around with a rather amused air.

ANGLE TO PAINTING

A larger than life-size painting of Pamela Morris, indirectly lighted. She stands beside a pedestal which bears an urn, in a garden, looking very young, very radiant, very lovely. There is a quality about the eyes that interests Jordan as he ENTERS SCENE to view her.

CLOSE SHOT—JORDAN

Studying the painting.

CLOSE ON PAINTING

Jordan examines the media, touches it, leans close to the artist's signature, looks at it intently.

INSERT—ARTIST'S SIGNATURE

It reads: BERTHOLD—1940

BACK TO SCENE

Jordan straightening, speaking to himself with a wry smile and a nod:

> JORDAN
> Nineteen forty.

ANGLE PAST GRAND PIANO IN F.G.

and TOWARD Jordan as he turns from the painting and strolls casually toward the piano where several framed pictures have been placed. He looks at them. They are all photographs of Pamela Morris. The SOUND of WATER SLOSHING O.S. makes him looks past the piano.

ANOTHER ANGLE—TOWARD FRENCH DOORS

They are open. Jordan walks toward them.

EXT. TERRACE—ANGLE TOWARD DOORS

Jordan walks through them, up to the balcony rail, stops, puts his hands on the rail, stares down, the edge of contempt he has exhibited all along vanishing with surprising suddenness.

P.O.V. SHOT—SWIMMING POOL

Olympic-sized, the maid standing at the pool edge, PAMELA MORRIS emerging from the pool in a flesh-colored swimsuit. She takes off her bathing cap and her hair falls about her shoulders. She looks in her 20s. She and the maid, who hands her a towel, speak in PANTOMIME. Miss Morris is one magnificently beautiful woman, and she moves with feline grace. The maid nods to the house, Miss Morris glancing toward it, CAMERA ZOOMING IN on her face.

CLOSE SHOT—JORDAN

Transfixed, pleased, attracted.

> SERLING'S VOICE
> Jordan Herrick, syndicated columnist whose work appears in more than a hundred newspapers, by nature a cynic, a disbeliever, caught for the moment by a vision.

SHOT—SERLING

> SERLING
> He knows the vision he has seen is no dream ...She is Pamela Morris, renowned movie star whose name is a household word and whose face is known to millions...What Mr. Herrick does *not* know is that he has also just looked into the face of the Twilight Zone.

FADE OUT

FADE IN:

INT. MANSION—CLOSE ON PORTRAIT—DAY

CAMERA DRAWS BACK to INCLUDE Jordan, who stares at the painting.

ANGLE TO DOORWAY

Pamela appears there, shockingly beautiful, though her attire is simple: slacks, thongs, shirtwaist.

                    PAMELA
        Mr. Herrick?

ANGLE TO JORDAN

Turning, drawing in his breath at the sight of her. His professional indifference then masks his emotions.

                    JORDAN
        Yes.

SHOT—PAMELA—MOVING

All charm. Jordan joins her in the center of the room.

                    PAMELA
        I've kept you waiting.

                    JORDAN
        Not at all…I mean, it doesn't matter.

She takes his hand, starts off with him.

                    PAMELA
        It *does* matter, and I'm sorry.

ANGLE TO COUCH

Where Pamela sinks to one part of it, Jordan to another.

>   PAMELA
> But I do love the pool.
>   (a warm smile)
> Am I forgiven?

>   JORDAN
> Certainly. It's I who should ask you to excuse
> the intrusion.

She puts out a hand to touch his arm, smiling.

>   PAMELA
> Please relax. I think you're very nice.

CLOSE SHOT—JORDAN

Forcing himself to be blunt.

>   JORDAN
> Miss Morris, just how old are you?

CLOSE SHOT—PAMELA

Lifting her head back, laughing, then looking to Jordan with good humor.

>   PAMELA
> I must say, you are a direct man, Mr. Herrick.

TWO SHOT—PAMELA AND JORDAN

He is surprised by her reaction.

>   JORDAN
> You're not offended?

                    PAMELA
          Should I be? I have my producers, my directors.
          You have your editors. They are all
          very demanding.
                         (beat)
          Besides, a woman in my position must have
          no secrets.

                    JORDAN
          I'm relieved to hear that. I was afraid—

                    PAMELA
          You have nothing to fear here.

Jordan is very intense. Pamela smiles at him until his face brightens with an answering smile. Then:

                    PAMELA
          That's better.
                         (beat)
          Now suppose you tell me how old you think
          I am.

                    JORDAN
          That's hardly fair.

                    PAMELA
          Oh, come on, now.

The CAMERA DRAWS BACK as Pamela gets up, pirouetting before him. He is unable to take his eyes from her. She makes a final turn, faces him.

                    PAMELA
          Well?

Jordan swallows, not knowing what to say. Finally:

                    JORDAN
                 (meaning it)
            You're—very beautiful.

                    PAMELA
            That wasn't the question.

                    JORDAN
            You look no older than—

His eyes flick to the O.S. painting. She turns.

ANGLE TO PAINTING

Pamela ENTERS SCENE to look at it soberly.

                    PAMELA
            I was but a child when I posed for Berthold.

Jordan ENTERS SCENE to stand beside her.

                    PAMELA
            I was frightened of him...the world was so
            bright and new to me and he was so wildly
            creative...I'd never met anyone like him.
            It was his genius that enabled him to project
            the flowering of a fragile blossom...

As O.S. BATTLE makes them turn toward it.

ANGLE TO DOORWAY

The maid rolls in a tray with a teakettle, miniature coffee urn, cups, dishes, and silverware. CAMERA FOLLOWS as she moves to the couch, being joined by Pamela and Jordan, who sit, the maid staring to set out cups and saucers.

                    PAMELA
            Tea or coffee, Mr. Herrick?

                    JORDAN
            Coffee, please.

TWO SHOT—PAMELA AND JORDAN

                    PAMELA
            Would you like something in it—cognac,
            whiskey?

                    JORDAN
            No, thank you.
                         (to maid)
            I'll take it black.

                    PAMELA
            I thought newspaper people were heavy
            drinkers.

                    JORDAN
            It's a myth.

They both look O.S., Jordan getting up.

ANGLE TO DOORWAY

Mrs. Draper appears. Despite the difference in ages, she bears a resemblance to Pamela and has much of her vitality. She comes in.

ANGLE TO COUCH

Mrs. Draper approaching, Pamela and Jordan on their feet, the maid setting out three services, Jordan eyeing the old woman curiously.

                    PAMELA
            My mother, Mrs. Draper...Jordan Herrick.

> JORDAN
> How do you do.

> PAMELA
> He's a newspaperman, Mother.

> MRS. DRAPER
> How do you do.

> JORDAN
> (with wonderment)
> It's remarkable, the resemblance between you two.

> PAMELA
> (edge of sharpness)
> Sit down, Mother. Have your tea.

ANGLE TO CHAIR

Mrs. Draper moves to it stiffly, sits to stare at Jordan O.S. as the maid hands her her tea.

> PAMELA'S VOICE
> With my mother it is tea at this precise time every afternoon. With me, it's coffee.

TWO SHOT—PAMELA AND JORDAN

Being handed their coffee by the maid.

> JORDAN
> (to Mrs. Draper)
> Mrs. Draper, you must feel proud to have a daughter as famous as Pamela Morris.

                    PAMELA
                   (quickly)
   Mother never did wholly approve of my career.

Jordan looks to Mrs. Draper for her reaction.

THREE SHOT—FAVORING MRS. DRAPER

The maid moving off in the B.G.

                 MRS. DRAPER
   Believe me, Mr. Herrick, I had little choice
   in the matter.

Pamela covers Jordan's hand with hers, an action noticed by Mrs. Draper and Jordan.

                    PAMELA
   She thinks I'm too headstrong.

                 MRS. DRAPER
   Dedicated is the word.
                    (beat)
   You still are, Pamela.

                    JORDAN
   Tell me, was your daughter always as beautiful
   as she is right now?

                 MRS. DRAPER
                   (gravely)
   Always.

                    JORDAN
   Now there is loyalty.

                 MRS. DRAPER
   As a matter of fact, Mr. Herrick, it is the truth.

> JORDAN
> (with a glance to Pamela)
> Perhaps from the mother I might learn the real age of the daughter.

> PAMELA
> Isn't age relative?
> (coquettish)
> Besides, didn't I promise to reveal all to you, Mr. Herrick?

> MRS. DRAPER
> Mr. Herrick—

> PAMELA
> (edge of harshness)
> Mother, you've finished your tea, haven't you? Would you mind seeing if Charlotte has things under control in the kitchen?

For a moment Pamela and Mrs. Draper eye each other, then Mrs. Draper puts down her cup and saucer, gets up, Jordan rising also.

> JORDAN
> I'm pleased to have met you, Mrs. Draper.

> MRS. DRAPER
> (with deliberate finality)
> I hope I see you again, Mr. Herrick.

She exits.

TWO SHOT—PAMELA AND JORDAN

Looking after the departing Mrs. Draper.

> PAMELA
> Forgive her, but she's getting old.

                    JORDAN
          I had thought she might tell me a few things I
          could use.

                    PAMELA
          No. Her mind wanders. Her memory becomes
          increasingly distorted.
                         (change of pace)
          Shall we finish our coffee on the terrace? I'm
          sure there's a breeze out there.

She reaches for his free hand as they get up.

EXT. TERRACE—ANGLE TO DOORS

Pamela and Jordan coming through them, to sit in chairs beside a small table where they put their coffee.

                    PAMELA
          Isn't it lovely out here? I often sit here by the
          hour watching the birds and the clouds…At
          night I watch the stars.

                    JORDAN
          It's nice.

                    PAMELA
                    (turning to him)
          But that isn't what interests you—my nocturnal
          habits, how I dream out here.

                    JORDAN
          It'll fit into the story I'm doing, but—

                    PAMELA
          The question of age is the big thing, isn't it?

CLOSE TWO SHOT—PAMELA AND JORDAN

Pamela looking at him with a wistful smile.

> PAMELA
> I am thirty-eight, Jordan…May I call you Jordan?

> JORDAN
> Of course.

> PAMELA
> Is thirty-eight terribly old?

> JORDAN
> The years have never been kinder to anyone.

> PAMELA
> (hand over his)
> What a nice thing to say!

> JORDAN
> I mean it.

He does mean it, but suddenly he frowns, withdraws his hand, reaches into a pocket, takes out a notebook, opens it, looks at it, his frown deepening.

> PAMELA
> What do you have there?

> JORDAN
> Some notes. Dates mostly.

> PAMELA
> Do they concern me?

> JORDAN
> If you are thirty-eight…

                    PAMELA
                    (cuts in)
    I know! You've read something—a column
    by one of those stupid, jealous women!

                    JORDAN
                    (doggedly)
    If you are thirty-eight, how could you have
    played the female lead in a movie in nineteen
    thirty-five?

INT. LIVING ROOM—ANGLE TO DOORWAY

Mrs. Draper comes in. We HEAR Pamela's silvery laughter from the terrace. She looks toward it.

P.O.V. SHOT—THE FRENCH DOORS AND TERRACE

Pamela and Jordan seated there, their backs to the living room.

                    PAMELA'S VOICE
    I can't believe it! Jordan Herrick taken in by
    the printed word!

EXT. TERRACE—PAMELA AND JORDAN

                    PAMELA
                    (amused)
    Tell me, do you always believe everything you
    read?

                    JORDAN
                    (referring to notes)
    The movie was *Trails West*.

                    PAMELA
    Darling, it couldn't have been me. I would
    have had to be nine years old, don't you see?

It's an old mistake. I've run across it before.

> JORDAN
> According to our files, your co-star was John Bradley. You were in love with him.

> PAMELA
> (smiles)
> I never even met him! Your files are in error. It happens, you know.

CLOSE ON PAMELA

Turning to look wistfully across the yard.

> PAMELA
> Nineteen thirty-five…Why, I don't believe I'd even seen a movie yet. We were poor, we lived in Iowa, my father's business was failing…

INT. LIVING ROOM—ANGLE TO MRS. DRAPER

She stands beside the French doors, listening.

> PAMELA'S VOICE
> It wasn't until nineteen forty that I set out for Hollywood, a star-struck girl in her teens, following the trail blazed by so many hopefuls.
> (beat)
> I was lucky.

EXT. TERRACE—PAMELA AND JORDAN

Jordan refers to his notes.

JORDAN
You must have been. You made *Queen of the Nile* with Charles Danforth in nineteen forty.
(beat)
You were fourteen.

PAMELA
Juliet was twelve.

JORDAN
But fourteen...

PAMELA
Is that so much harder to believe than my being thirty-eight today? You see, no one *knew* I was only fourteen. I matured early.

JORDAN
I take it the picture inspired the decor...
(he gestures in the direction of the living room)

PAMELA
(smiling)
Yes. I suppose it's kind of silly, but—it was my first big break, and...well, I'm just glad it wasn't one of those horror pictures, or I'd probably have the place full of caskets.

They both laugh.

PAMELA
(continued)
But, really, you know the fact is that I still feel fourteen...No, with you sitting there I feel new and breathless and just twenty-one. I want to live, Jordan. I want to savor all there is in this life. Is it wrong for me to feel this way?

>   JORDAN
> No.

She draws away.

>   PAMELA
> I'm being foolish, saying these things to you.

>   JORDAN
>   (rising quickly)
> On the contrary.

ANGLE TO RAILING

Pamela moves to it, looks morosely out over the yard as he moves to her side.

>   PAMELA
> It's just that—I so seldom get the chance to
> speak my mind, to air my dreams.
>   (turning to him)
> You are so understanding.

She puts a hand on his cheek, moves very close.

>   PAMELA
> So simpatico…

Her lips invite his kiss. He takes her in his arms.

INT. LIVING ROOM—CLOSE ON MRS. DRAPER

She turns from watching them, leans against the wall, troubled, agitated.

EXT. TERRACE—PAMELA AND JORDAN

They are in an embrace. She breaks away, turns away.

PAMELA
What must you think of me!

JORDAN
(turns her to him)
I wanted to kiss you from the very first moment I saw you.

She brings out a small hankie, brushes his now-rouged lips with it, smiling, saying in a honeyed voice:

PAMELA
You're very sweet, very real.
(now sadly)
But you really must go.

JORDAN
Why?

PAMELA
(almost a pout)
Because I say so. But we'll see each other again, if you like…

JORDAN
What about tonight? Dinner?

PAMELA
(starting away)
Very well.
(holding out her hand)
Shall we say—eight o'clock?

JORDAN
Eight o'clock.

They leave the terrace, hand in hand.

EXT. MANSION—MED. LONG SHOT TO FRONT DOOR—
DAY

The front door opens, Jordan coming out, spring in his step, eagerness and expectation in his face.

ANGLE PAST SPORTS CAR IN F.G.

and TOWARD the approaching Jordan. He comes around to this side of the car, whistling cheerfully.

              MRS. DRAPER'S VOICE
                  (hoarse whisper)
    Mr. Herrick!

He stops, looks around, sees Mrs. Draper O.S., starts for her, the CAMERA MOVING AHEAD to where she stands by a pillar so she cannot be seen from the house. Jordan joins her.

TWO SHOT—MRS. DRAPER AND JORDAN

                    JORDAN
    Mrs. Draper.

She eyes him steadily.

                  MRS. DRAPER
    Mr. Herrick, you are a fine young man.

                    JORDAN
    Thank you, Mrs. Draper.

                  MRS. DRAPER
    It is not an idle compliment.
                    (beat)
    Are you going to see her again?

                    JORDAN
          Why, yes. We're going out to dinner together,
          tonight.

She moves to him, puts a hand on his arm, her eyes full of appeal, CAMERA TIGHTENING the SHOT.

                    MRS. DRAPER
          No. No, you must not do that. You mustn't
          see her again.

                    JORDAN
          But why?

                    MRS. DRAPER
          She's older than you think.

                    JORDAN
          Mrs. Draper, she *told* me how old she is.

ANOTHER ANGLE

Mrs. Draper turning away toward CAMERA, her lips curled.

                    MRS. DRAPER
          Yes, I know. Thirty-eight.

                    JORDAN
          Just how old is she?

                    MRS. DRAPER
          Mr. Herrick, you wouldn't believe me if I told
          you how old I think she is.

                    JORDAN
          Think she is! Don't you *know?*

> MRS. DRAPER
> (turning)
> No. Not really.
>
> JORDAN
> But—you're her mother!
>
> MRS. DRAPER
> No...I'm not her mother.

CLOSE SHOT—MRS. DRAPER

A long, hard look at him. Then softly:

> MRS. DRAPER
> I'm her daughter.

FADE OUT

FADE IN:

EXT. LA CIENEGA RESTAURANT ROW—NIGHT

The street bustles with traffic.

DISSOLVE THROUGH TO:

TWO SHOT—PAMELA AND JORDAN IN CAR—NIGHT

In Jordan's sports car, both in evening attire, Jordan looking very handsome, Pamela very beautiful.

DISSOLVE THROUGH TO:

INT. RESTAURANT—ANGLE TO MAITRE D'—NIGHT

Pamela and Jordan move to him, the maitre d' smiling at Pamela, bowing, greeting her in PANTOMIME, moving off with them.

DISSOLVE THROUGH TO:

TWO SHOT—PAMELA AND JORDAN AT A TABLE

Pamela pausing with her dinner and her talk to look at Jordan, smiling, putting out a hand to him, Jordan managing a smile in return.

DISSOLVE THROUGH TO:

TWO SHOT—PAMELA AND JORDAN IN CAR—NIGHT

She leans her head against Jordan's shoulder, closes her eyes happily.

DISSOLVE THROUGH TO:

INT. NIGHT CLUB—ANGLE TO TABLE—NIGHT

A cozy corner, Pamela and Jordan sitting with drinks before them. Pamela's hand covers his.

ANOTHER ANGLE—CLOSER

She smiles at him blissfully.

> PAMELA
> I don't know when I've had such a wonderful time.

A young WOMAN comes INTO SCENE with an autograph book, stands awkwardly by until Pamela slides her eyes to her.

> WOMAN
> Miss Morris?

> PAMELA
> Yes?

                    WOMAN
            May I have your autograph?

                    PAMELA
            Of course, dear.

The woman hands her the book and a pen, but steals furtive glances at Jordan as Pamela signs. Pamela returns the book with a smile.

                    WOMAN
            Thank you, Miss Morris.

She moves off.

CLOSE ON PAMELA

Turning back to Jordan, smiling, but with a trace of concern.

                    PAMELA
            Darling, you've been quiet all evening.

SHOT—JORDAN

Looking down at his drink, troubled.

                    PAMELA
            What is it?

Jordan's eyes come up, he smiles wryly.

                    JORDAN
            Something your mother said. I don't believe it.
                    (then slowly)
            But it sticks in my mind.

                    PAMELA
            Tell me.

JORDAN

She said—you are her mother.

PAMELA

Her mother!
(now earnestly)
Jordan, you must believe me. My mother is—disturbed.

SHOT—PAMELA

Very upset at the memory, she tries to compose herself.

PAMELA

It's that she—feels responsible for my father's death…They were returning from a party ten years ago…she was driving…the car went off the road…Father was killed.

TWO SHOT—PAMELA AND JORDAN

JORDAN

I'm sorry.

PAMELA

Since then…she's been…suspicious, furtive, imagining all sorts of terrible things. I've tried to help her, but the doctors say it's hopeless. It's senility. She should be put away, I know, but—

JORDAN

Don't torture yourself.

She brightens, tries to smile through her tears.

PAMELA
All right. We'll discuss something else. I've told you about me, and now you know about my mother. What about you?

JORDAN
In comparison to yours, my life has been very dull—up to now.

PAMELA
Where did you grow up?

JORDAN
Chicago. I still live there, work there.

PAMELA
I've played Chicago. The Wells Theater. Is it always cold in Chicago?

JORDAN
Only in the wintertime.

They both laugh.

DISSOLVE:

EXT. MANSION—FULL SHOT—NIGHT

The sports car moves into the driveway.

ANGLE TO VERANDA

The sports car moving to a stop before it.

TWO SHOT—PAMELA AND JORDAN IN THE CAR

Pamela looking at him fondly.

> PAMELA
> It's been heavenly, Jordan. Every minute of it.

She moves to him, kisses him, then breaks away.

> PAMELA
> It's late…Shall I see you tomorrow?

> JORDAN
> (reaching for her)
> Wild horses—

With a laugh she eludes him, slides out of the car, blows him a kiss.

> PAMELA
> Till tomorrow, darling.

She moves off.

CLOSE ON JORDAN

His eyes narrow slightly as he looks after her. We HEAR the CLICK of her heels on the porch.

ANGLE TO DOOR

Pamela turning, waving, opening the door, going in.

ANGLE TO CAR

Jordan starting it, driving it off.

DISSOLVE THROUGH TO:

EXT. STREET—ANGLE PAST PHONE BOOTH IN F.G.—NIGHT

and TOWARD the approaching sports car. Jordan drives up to the curb, gets out of the car, moves to the phone booth.

INT. PHONE BOOTH—JORDAN

He closes the door behind him, deposits a dime, dials the operator. After a moment:

> JORDAN
> I want to place a collect call to Chicago.

INT. NEWSPAPER OFFICE—MED. SHOT—KRUEGER

A heavyset man, sixty-five or older. He sits in his shirt sleeves at a universal desk, editing wire copy. The phone before him rings. He picks it up.

> KRUEGER
> Kreuger.
> (instantly alive)
> Jordie! I'm glad you called. I've got another job for you—that is, if you're through playing around with that little Hollywood femme fatale.

> JORDAN
> I'm not—not yet, anyway. Do something for me, Krueger—get out the file on a picture called *Queen of the Nile*.

> KRUEGER
> Which one?

> JORDAN
> What do you mean?

> KRUEGER
> (smiling)
> Well, you're a little young for this, I guess...

but they made two of 'em. First one silent, I
think—around nineteen twenty, maybe earlier.

JORDAN
Get them both. I'll hang on.

INT. PHONE BOOTH—NIGHT—CLOSE ON JORDAN

He takes out a cigarette, lights it.

KRUEGER
You there?

JORDAN
Yeah. What's the name of the girl who starred
in the original?

KRUEGER
Constance Taylor. Anyway, she starred in
most of it... There was some kind of accident
during the shooting. A cave-in at the tomb...
in Egypt somewhere. They never found her.

JORDAN
Got a picture of Miss Taylor?

KRUEGER
Yeah.

JORDAN
Compare it with a picture of Pamela Morris.

KRUEGER

He goes through the two files, selects two photographs.

JORDAN
Well?

                    KRUEGER
    They look alike...but they played the same
    part, with the same make-up, same type of
    costume...

INSERT—THE TWO PHOTOGRAPHS

Revealing unmistakably the twin-like similarity between the two.

CLOSE SHOT—JORDAN

                    JORDAN
    Listen, the old Wells Theater. When did they
    tear that down?

                    KRUEGER
    Sometime in the twenties. Why? Jordie, *why?*

                    JORDAN
    You'll find out pretty soon. Meantime, find
    out about the men who were involved with
    Pamela Morris...send me every press release,
    every clipping you have on her. And fast.

                    KRUEGER
    Sounds interesting.

                    JORDAN
    It may sound fantastic.

                                        DISSOLVE:

INT. MANSION—ANGLE THROUGH WINDOW—DAY

SHOOTING through the French doors to the swimming pool where Pamela splashes about. The CAMERA DRAWS BACK to show Jordan watching her from this side of the doors. He turns.

ANGLE PAST MRS. DRAPER IN F.G.

and TOWARD Jordan as he approaches her. Mrs. Draper leafs through the file of papers we last saw before Krueger in the Chicago newspaper office. She is seated in a chair.

				JORDAN
	Well?

Mrs. Draper leans back, the folder in her lap.

				MRS. DRAPER
		It's all true, Mr. Herrick. It's all true.
				(urgently)
		But don't show it to her! Leave here at once.

Ignoring her plea, Jordan picks up one of the clippings, yellow with age, shows it to her.

				JORDAN
	Is this Pamela?

				MRS. DRAPER
		Yes, yes. Please, Mr. Herrick. You don't
		know how it is.

He looks at it.

INSERT—CLIPPING

The date reads: Jan. 12, 1923. It is a picture of Pamela Morris and a man in a love scene. The overline reads: AT THE WELLS ON ROAD SHOW TOUR. The names beneath are: Gladys Gregory and Kester Roberts. The large cutlines read: New at the Wells Theater this week are Gladys Gregory and Kester Roberts, fresh from their Broadway success of "Honeymoon Deferred."

TWO SHOT—JORDAN AND MRS. DRAPER

Jordan putting the clipping back, picking up the folder.

> MRS. DRAPER
> She had many different names.

> JORDAN
> But she herself hasn't changed in forty years.

> MRS. DRAPER
> Forty years? At least seventy years. The sum total of my life.
> (beat)
> You can't imagine what it was like…to see her always so fresh and beautiful, while my mirrored image grew seared and yellowed with age…How I longed to see a wrinkle—just one!—in that baby-skin face…But it stayed young, and it was I who grew bent and gnarled, withered by the press of years…Is it any wonder I hate her so?

TWO SHOT—JORDAN AND MRS. DRAPER

Mrs. Draper getting up, moving to the painting, Jordan behind her, CAMERA FOLLOWING. She looks at it.

> MRS. DRAPER
> Look at her, Mr. Herrick. And then go.

> JORDAN
> How old is she, really?

> MRS. DRAPER
> She is ageless…Perhaps she's eternal.

> JORDAN
> What is her secret?

MRS. DRAPER
(turning away)
What woman would not sell her soul to know?
(gesturing)
It has something to do with the motif in this room—the beetles.

JORDAN
(looking around)
The scarabaeid beetle...the Egyptian symbol for everlasting life.

ANOTHER ANGLE

Mrs. Draper moving to the couch, Jordan following.

JORDAN
Mrs. Draper, if you hate her so—

MRS. DRAPER
Why do I stay?
(beat)
What else could I do? After Pamela and my husband—

She breaks off, a look of fright coming into her eyes.

JORDAN
Go on. Tell me the rest.

MRS. DRAPER
No. I cannot. You must go!

JORDAN
What about those other men—John Bradley, Charles Danforth, Wesley Harrington—

                    MRS. DRAPER
                     (terrified)
            Don't ask about them!

                      JORDAN
            Mrs. Draper, listen to me—

                   PAMELA'S VOICE
            Mr. Herrick.

Jordan turns, Mrs. Draper looks frightenedly O.S.

ANGLE TO DOORWAY

Pamela moving in, clad in a form-fitting robe.

                      PAMELA
            How nice of you to drop in like this!

TWO SHOT—MRS. DRAPER AND JORDAN

Pamela joining them, exuding charm, looking at Mrs. Draper.

                      PAMELA
            Has my mother been entertaining you?

The maid rolls in the tea tray in the B.G. Jordan stares at Pamela. Mrs. Draper sits rigid. Pamela smiles sweetly at her.

                      PAMELA
            What wild tales have you been spinning,
            Mother?

                      JORDAN
            I don't think they're wild tales at all.

Pamela flashes him a glance. The maid moves the tray between them.

                    JORDAN
        For example, the Wells Theater, where you
        played, was torn down in the twenties.

MED. SHOT—PAMELA

Turning, taking a chair as the maid pours.

                    PAMELA
                    (coldly)
        You may leave us, Mother. Charlotte will
        prepare your tea in your room.

GROUP

Mrs. Draper getting up, the maid moving off.

                    MRS. DRAPER
        Pamela…please.

                    PAMELA
                    (sharply)
        I want to speak to Mr. Herrick alone.

LOW ANGLE PAST COFFEE CUP IN F.G.

and TOWARD Mrs. Draper and Jordan. Mrs. Draper moves off, Jordan looking after her. Pamela's HAND comes INTO FRAME. The fingers drop a white pill into the coffee. The CAMERA RISES, MOVES BACK to INCLUDE Pamela. In the B.G., the maid waits at the door for Mrs. Draper, who turns for a last look at them before going out, the maid following, closing the door.

                    PAMELA
        Your coffee, Mr. Herrick.

She pushes the coffee cup across to him, takes the other cup. Jordan takes the coffee.

                          PAMELA
                    You were saying?

Jordan sips the coffee, nods to the folder beside him.

                          JORDAN
               I've compiled quite a dossier on you.

He takes another sip of coffee.

SHOT—PAMELA

Unperturbed, coolly sipping her coffee.

                          PAMELA
               What is it you want—money?

                          JORDAN
                    No. Just the truth.

He runs a finger under his collar.

MED. SHOT—PAMELA

Smiling sweetly.

                          PAMELA
               And you shall have it, Mr. Herrick.

She puts down her coffee cup, gets up, moves off.

SHOT—JORDAN

He puts down the coffee, gets out a handkerchief, wipes his perspiring forehead, frowns as he tries to focus his eyes.

ANGLE TO WALL SAFE

Pamela moves to the large silvered beetle escutcheon, tilts it to one side, exposing a dial. She works the combination, opens it, brings out a glass box.

ANGLE TO JORDAN

Pamela joining him, putting the glass box on the coffee table. Jordan sways a little, says thickly:

> JORDAN
> What—is it?

> PAMELA
> A rare Egyptian scarab, Mr. Herrick. The secret of eternity.

CLOSE ON BOX

The large beetle inside moves around. Jordan's bleary face ENTERS FRAME. He blinks his eyes, looks up.

ANOTHER ANGLE

> JORDAN
> Where...did...you...?

> PAMELA
> (smiles)
> Get it? From the Pharohs who understood its power....

> JORDAN
> Pharohs...? *You?*

> PAMELA
> (her sweetest smile)
> I *told* you, Mr. Herrick, I was once Queen of the Nile.

JORDAN

You are...?
(he can no longer speak)

TWO SHOT—PAMELA AND JORDAN

Jordan looking up at her smiling countenance, understanding coming too late. He tries to stand, but falls back to the couch. Pamela quickly moves to the box.

CLOSE ON JORDAN'S CHEST

Pamela moves the box to his chest, opens his shirt, sets the box down, slides out the bottom lid.

EXTREME CLOSE-UP—THE BEETLE

It inserts its eager proboscis into the flesh.

SHOT—PAMELA'S FACE

Expectant.

ANGLE TO JORDAN AND PAMELA

She slides the bottom of the box on, takes it from his chest, moves to the couch, bares her leg, puts the box there, slides out the bottom plate, staring at the beetle.

CLOSE SHOT—JORDAN'S FACE

It loses its glow, becomes sallow, leathery, wrinkled and withered with age, finally being reduced to a skull, and then the skull crumbles, falling in on itself, leaving nothing but dust and finally only a rumpled pile of clothing.

ANGLE TO WALL SAFE

Pamela putting the glass box in, closing the safe door; the SOUND of a DOOR closing O.S. is HEARD. Pamela swings the beetle escutcheon closed, looks O.S.

MED. SHOT—MRS. DRAPER

Staring with horror at the remains of Jordan, being joined by an irate Pamela. She is very ugly and unpleasant.

                  PAMELA
    I told you never to come in until I call you,
    Viola. If you want to live another day—

She breaks off at the O.S. SOUND of the heavy front door KNOCKER. Pamela and Mrs. Draper exchange startled glances. Pamela pushes Mrs. Draper toward what is left of Jordan.

                  PAMELA
      You know what to do. Quickly.

She starts for the doorway, smoothing her robe, composing herself.

REVERSE ANGLE

Pamela opening the door, stepping out.

HER P.O.V.—MAID AND MR. JACKSON

Jackson is a good-looking young man of about thirty, at the moment taken aback by the beauty of Pamela. The maid closes the door behind him, starts off.

SHOT—PAMELA—MOVING

All sweetness and light as she joins Jackson.

                  PAMELA
      You must be Mr. Jackson.

> JACKSON
> Yes. I called the other day—

> PAMELA
> And I told you to come out when you could. Did you think I'd forget?

ANOTHER ANGLE

Pamela takes his hand, moves with him to the door to the living room.

> PAMELA
> Come. We'll have coffee in the living room.

They go through the door. As they enter the living room:

> SERLING'S VOICE
> Everybody knows Pamela Morris, the beautiful and eternally young movie star. Or does she have another name even more famous—an Egyptian name from centuries past? It's best not to be too curious, lest you wind up like Jordan Herrick—a pile of dust and old clothing discarded in the endless eternity of…the Twilight Zone.

FADE OUT

Afterword: A Touch of Strange
by George Clayton Johnson

Looking at these *Twilight Zone* scripts that Jerry Sohl ghosted to help Charles Beaumont I am brought to recall how uncanny Jerry's ability was to take a fresh idea, join with others to verbally plot out a television episode, and, without taking any apparent notes, promptly reproduce the story for the camera on 8 ½ x 11 pages in the form of a complete teleplay filled with rich dialogue.

It was a marvelous talent and one that should have been put to greater use.

At least, I thought so at the time.

I vividly remember walking along the curved corridors of the starship *Enterprise* with Jerry Sohl, Theodore Sturgeon and Richard Matheson, talking about the future. We'd each been hired by Gene Roddenberry to write episodes for his new series *Star Trek,* and been given the run of the premises.

We were taking advantage of his generosity to familiarize ourselves with the workings of the ship—a grand tour of the starship's standing sets.

Jerry was writing "The Corbomite Maneuver," Sturgeon, "Amok Time," Matheson, "The Enemy Within," and I was working on "The Mantrap."

However, as we walked along, instead of being caught up in the fantasy of being aboard the spaceship, we were still lamenting the death of Rod Serling's *Twilight Zone* series.

As we looked into the forced perspective of the engineering section, which I noticed that in reality, seen as a prop, could be fitted into a garage, Jerry brought up an idea we had discussed earlier—why not team up to get a series of our own, some kind of half-hour fantasy series like *The Twilight Zone?* We could hire all of our friends to write the scripts. It was a grand idea.

We discussed names, all friends of Charles Beaumont. William F. Nolan, of course, and Frank M. Robinson and Ray Russell and John Tomerlin. What about Harlan Ellison, or George Bamber, or Ray Bradbury himself?

The idea was beginning to shape up.

We could hire an independent agent to represent us as a package while keeping our own representation for all other matters.

Jerry wanted this to work.

He pointed out how many books and stories we had written between ourselves that we could draw from, and how suited we were to guarantee the ability to write, between ourselves, all of the scripts if necessary. Each of us still had a file full of *Twilight Zone* ideas.

At first Richard Matheson was skeptical. He was doing all right by himself.

Sturgeon hadn't shown his cards—he was receptive but uncommitted. Exactly what would the show be like? How would it be different from *The Twilight Zone,* or better?

We brainstormed the problem.

We decided it would be a series of short stories, adapted for television, with a host/narrator whose presence would be felt throughout the dramatization, instead of the accustomed introduction and epilogue.

The Narrator would talk to a character, as a voice-over, much in the manner of a conscience, instead of to the audience as Rod had done.

It would be a different way of intensifying the story by providing an *omniscient author* who sees beneath the surface of what the audience is seeing by his insights into the protagonist's behavior and attitude and by his sardonic tone, a literary tool sadly lacking in television drama but highly respected by the world's great novelists.

They would be stories of psychological terror, very realistically staged though done in a minimalist style.

Jerry suggested we call the series *A Touch of Strange,* a Sturgeon title.

The stories would be brief, disturbing and moral. They would be what Sturgeon called "wisdom fiction."

By this time both Sturgeon and Matheson had caught fire with the idea.

During the next few weeks over dinner together at the Jolly Roger restaurant near Matheson's home we worked out the details of what we were prepared to offer as a company.

We hired a lawyer to draw up the papers for The Green Hand—a California Corporation. It took Sturgeon to remind us that in Western parlance a "green hand" is a raw beginner, which certainly seemed appropriate.

We appointed Gus Elwell, a young agent who had worked for the Jerry Adler Agency, to go out and shop us as a team.

Gus quickly arranged a meeting for us with Charles Pratt of Bing Crosby Productions, who had offices on the Paramount lot.

Charles saw the vision at once. He understood perfectly what we were talking about. He offered to hire us to put together a written proposal for *A Touch of Strange* to present to the networks. Should the proposal sell to a network we would enter into an agreement for us to furnish the scripts.

Jubilant, we went off to fashion a sales document in the form of a half-dozen stories and a proposed format in which to imbed the stories. We chose Richard Matheson's "Button, Button" to be our pilot.

Together we wrote a description of the show we had in mind. We hired an artist to make us a few sketches we thought might be useful in visualizing the program (titles in various styles to suggest the eerie nature of the program and the looming aspect of the Narrator), and delivered it all to Bing Crosby Productions.

Charles Pratt was pleased. He promptly shot it over to ABC.

Within a couple of weeks we had an appointment to meet with a Vice-President in Charge of Development.

The man turned out to be Michael Eisner, along with another young man who didn't contribute much except to vigorously agree to everything that Michael said.

It was apparent at once that to Michael we were small potatoes. He had much more important things on his mind.

All four of us took turns pitching the project with all the enthusiasm we could muster.

Charles Pratt was silent throughout.

Michael loved the stories. He thought it was an exciting project. The idea of a writing staff made a lot of sense and he had great respect for the Bing Crosby company and their ability to deliver the goods, with a nod to Charles Pratt who could sense the ax beginning to fall.

Michael praised Rod Serling but pointed out that Rod's show was barely a borderline success, existing from pick-up to pick-up, thirteen episodes at a time.

"No, gentlemen," he said, rising to his feet, signaling that the meeting was over. "It's too soon for *A Touch of Strange*."

He couldn't have been more genial and respectful, or charged with goodwill.

We had taken our shot and missed. Better luck next time.

Of us all, Charles Pratt was the greatest loser. There seemed to be no competition. In those days if one network turned down a project none of the other networks would touch it. Since the proposal was effectively dead, Matheson wanted "Button, Button" back, which we were quick to agree to, retrieving our own stories from the proposal as well, accepting our pay and turning our collective mind to other things.

Looking back I wonder if Michael Eisner was right and it was too soon to introduce another *Twilight Zone*-type series to the public?

Perhaps it is still too soon, even while it's too late.

Acknowledgements

As was the case with *Filet of Sohl,* Jerry Sohl's family was enormously helpful in seeing this book through to completion. Jean Sohl, Jerry's widow, not only provided necessary permissions, but also graciously consented to an interview about her husband's connection to *The Twilight Zone.* Jerry and Jean's children, Allan and Jennifer Sohl, were also supportive. Roger Anker and Marc Zicree assisted in locating scripts ("The New Exhibit" and "Queen of the Nile" are previously unpublished). Tony Albarella and Andrew Ramage provided ideas and enthusiasm. George Clayton Johnson is, as always, *sui generis.* Finally, a grateful tip of the hat to the indefatigable Ben Ohmart—for reasons too obvious to enumerate here.

C.C.
February 2004

Have You Seen The Wind?
Selected Stories and Poems
by William F. Nolan

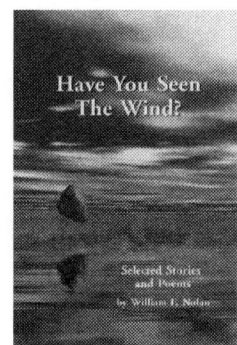

ISBN: 0-9714570-5-0   *$14.95*

With 75 books and over 300 anthology appearances to his credit, William F. Nolan (author of *Logan's Run*) is twice winner of the Edgar Allan Poe Special Award. Most recently, he accepted the International Guild's Living Legend Award for 2002.

This is the first collection of Nolan's horror fiction and verse to share a single volume. Six chilling tales of murder and madness, guns and obsession steam the pages of this haunting book, including "In Real Life," cited in *The Year's Best Fantasy and Horror*, and a brand new story written just for this collection: "Behind the Curtain."

Delve into Nolan's darkest worlds as he assembles tales of an ex-wife claiming revenge from beyond the grave… of an insane mind justifying the murder of his mate through the tall glass of a cold one… of a husband who refuses to stay dead… And top it all off with a celebration of this master's widely-praised poems, on topics ranging from Bradbury to Vienna, from Hammett to Hemingway.

COMMENTARY ON NOLAN'S PROSE

"William F. Nolan is a hell of a writer! I have real admiration for his stories."   —PETER STRAUB

"He makes a permanent dent in our memories. Nolan is able to create an atmosphere of ultimate terror, causing readers to live out his nightmares."   —RAY BRADBURY

"He's incredibly talented … Each of his stories is like a psychiatric session from which the reader comes away knowing more about the human condition, due to Nolan's fascination with the topography of emotional torment and his infallible rendering of the troubled psyche."
                                                                                —RICHARD CHRISTIAN MATHESON

AND ON HIS VERSE

"Nolan is a prime communicator … and although he writes only 'two or three' poems a year, he manages to communicate emotions better than most full-time poets."
                                                                                —SMALL PRESS REVIEW

___ YES, please send me ___ copies of *Have You Seen The Wind?* for just $14.95 each.

___ YES, I would like more information about your other publications.

Add $4 postage for up to 5 books. For non-US orders, please add $4 per book for airmail, in US funds. Payment must accompany all orders. Or buy online with Paypal at bearmanormedia.com.

My check or money order for $_____ is enclosed. Thank you.

NAME _____

ADDRESS _____

CITY/STATE/ZIP _____

EMAIL _____

Checks payable to: BearManor Media * P O Box 71426 * Albany, GA 31708
books@benohmart.com

FILET OF SOHL
The Classic Scripts and Stories of Jerry Sohl

Edited by Christopher Conlon

ISBN: 0-9714570-3-4   **$16.95**

JERRY SOHL (1913-2002) was one of the most successful science fiction, fantasy, and mystery writers of his time. A prolific author of novels (*Costigan's Needle, Point Ultimate*) and films (*Die, Monster, Die!* with Boris Karloff), he is perhaps best-known today for his teleplays for *The Twilight Zone, Star Trek, The Outer Limits,* and *Alfred Hitchcock Presents.* This is the first-ever collection of this master's scripts and stories!

Included in this volume:

★ Ten classic short tales, including two adapted for the legendary *Outer Limits*
★ Two never-seen scripts for *The Twilight Zone*
★ An intriguing story treatment for *Alfred Hitchcock Presents*
★ A powerful foreword by William F. Nolan
★ Essay-appreciations from George Clayton Johnson, Richard Matheson, and Marc Scott Zicree
★ Touching personal tributes from the author's son and daughter, Allan and Jennifer Sohl

For fans of classic science fiction, fantasy, and suspense—this is a book to savor!

___ YES, please send me ___ copies of *Filet of Sohl* for just $16.95 each.

___ YES, I would like more information about your other publications.

Add $4 postage for up to 5 books. For non-US orders, please add $4 per book for airmail, in US funds. Payment must accompany all orders. Or buy online with Paypal at bearmanormedia.com.

My check or money order for $_____ is enclosed. Thank you.

NAME _____

ADDRESS _____

CITY/STATE/ZIP _____

EMAIL _____

Checks payable to: BearManor Media * P O Box 71426 * Albany, GA 31708
books@benohmart.com

BearManor Media

OLD RADIO. OLD MOVIES. NEW BOOKS.

BearManor Media is a small press publishing Big books. Biographies, script collections, you name it. We love old time radio, voice actors and old films.

Current and upcoming projects include:

The Great Gildersleeve *Walter Tetley*
The Bickersons Scripts *Don Ameche*
The Baby Snooks Scripts *Guy Williams*
Information Please *Jane Kean*
The Life of Riley *Joel Rapp*
The Bickersons *Albert Salmi*
The Ritz Brothers *Peggy Ann Garner*
Paul Frees and many more!
Daws Butler

Write for a free catalog, or visit http://bearmanormedia.com today.

BearManor Media
P O Box 71426
Albany, GA 31708
books@benohmart.com

www.ingramcontent.com/pod-product-compliance
Lightning Source LLC
Chambersburg PA
CBHW022102160426
43198CB00008B/324